Heavenly Vaults

Heavenly Vaults

From Romanesque to Gothic
in European Architecture

DAVID STEPHENSON

PRINCETON ARCHITECTURAL PRESS

NEW YORK

Published by
Princeton Architectural Press
37 East Seventh Street
New York, New York 10003

For a free catalog of books, call 1.800.722.6657.
Visit our website at www.papress.com.

All photographs © David Stephenson (www.davidstephensonart.com),
represented by Julie Saul Gallery, New York

Editor: Nicola Bednarek
Designer: Jan Haux
Layout: Bree Anne Apperley

Special thanks to: Nettie Aljian, Sara Bader, Janet Behning, Becca Casbon, Carina Cha,
Penny (Yuen Pik) Chu, Carolyn Deuschle, Russell Fernandez, Pete Fitzpatrick, Wendy Fuller, Clare Jacobson,
Aileen Kwun, Nancy Eklund Later, Linda Lee, Laurie Manfra, John Myers, Katharine Myers,
Lauren Nelson Packard, Dan Simon, Andrew Stepanian, Jennifer Thompson, Paul Wagner,
Joseph Weston, and Deb Wood of Princeton Architectural Press
—Kevin C. Lippert, publisher

Library of Congress Cataloging-in-Publication Data
Stephenson, David, 1955–
Heavenly vaults : from Romanesque to Gothic in European architecture /
David Stephenson. — 1st ed.
p. cm.
ISBN 978-1-56898-840-5 (alk. paper)
1. Architectural photography—Europe. 2. Photography of interiors—Europe.
3. Vaults (Architecture), Medieval—Europe—Pictorial works. I. Title.
TR659.S738 2005
721'.43094'0902—dc22
2008054612

CONTENTS

Foreword

Human life is a conundrum. We not only live in a vast and complex outer world filled with cars, buildings, and people, but, simultaneously, in an equally intricate inner world of thoughts and feelings. Navigating between these two interconnected states of being, with varying degrees of success, we try to make sense of it all. What are we here for? What does it all mean?

The Judeo-Christian religions offered their medieval and Renaissance populace a comforting sense of certainty and resolution to these questions. Standing in their ancient churches, looking up at the vaulted ceilings, one can still feel the reassuring sense of order that these ecclesiastical buildings were designed to convey. The commanding vision of a cosmological order in which God ruled, nature provided, and we obeyed is inherent in the scale and symbolism of the buildings. A sense of awe, wonder, and obedience to the divine order was the only appropriate response when viewing the enormous stone vaults and decorated domes of the churches, which are illuminated by "God's light" pouring through the stained glass windows.

Even though the traditional systems that underpinned church architecture have lost their unequivocal power, David Stephenson's photographs capture the resonance of those times. More importantly his work also suggests that the feelings of aspiration, transcendence, and infinity these buildings evoke in the viewer have an ongoing relevance beyond the religious setting and help us understand who and what we are.

The sense of the sublime, which Stephenson captures powerfully here, has sustained his interest throughout a long and varied photographic career. As he has written, "While the subject of my photographs has shifted ... my art has remained essentially spiritual—for more than two decades I have been exploring a contemporary expression of the sublime—a transcendental experience of awe with the vast space and time of existence."[1] It is clear from looking at Stephenson's various groups of work that his creative trajectory is like an overlapping spiral; he returns repeatedly to themes and expands them but always with the impetus of the sublime as the generating core.

Of course, the concept of the sublime with which Stephenson engages is not new. It has a robust philosophical lineage stretching back to the eighteenth-century writings of Edmund Burke and Immanuel Kant, among others. With its attendant emotions of awe and terror, and its sense of infinity, the sublime was an experiential response to the majesty of untrammeled Nature and also informed much aesthetic theory. Today the period in which this philosophy held such a powerful grip on the imagination can seem like another universe. For most contemporary urban dwellers, the wilderness is seen in IMAX film format or narrated by David Attenborough on television rather than experienced first hand. Even looking at the stars—that traditional nightly reminder of the infinity of the universe—is muted, if not obliterated, by city lights. Our relationship to nature has been transformed; it is more common to think of nature as a harnessed resource that appears to be running out of steam instead of the traditional unlimited, divine, and all-powerful force.

Stephenson is fully aware of these shifts in consciousness, and his photographs of the natural world, in particular, express an appreciation of the delicate balance between land care and land use. Stephenson lives, in fact, in Tasmania, where such issues are of

1
David Stephenson, preface to *Sublime Space: Photographs by David Stephenson 1989–1998*, by Susan van Wyk (Melbourne: National Gallery of Victoria, 1998), 1.

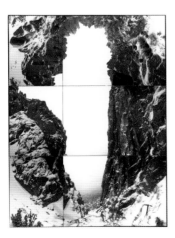

SELF PORTRAIT,
AVALANCHE COULOIR, 1985
From the series Composite Landscapes
Gelatin silver photograph, 100 x 80 cm

THE ICE NO. 1, 1992
From the series The Ice
Type C photograph, 100 x 145 cm

STARS 1996/1211, 1996
From the series Stars
Ilfochrome photograph, 100 x 100 cm

NEW SYNAGOGUE
Szeged, Hungary
From the series Domes
Type C photograph, 56 x 56 cm

great concern. This island state, located some 149 miles (240 kilometers) from mainland Australia's eastern seaboard, is a place where the demands of wilderness and industry often compete. We get a sense of these stresses in some of his earliest photographs, taken soon after he arrived in Tasmania in 1982. With pictorial references to the nineteenth-century American photographic panoramas of Timothy O'Sullivan and Carleton Watkins, Stephenson's disjointed panoramas represent a world in which nature is no longer unquestioningly considered a mute resource to serve our unending needs.

In the 1990s, the individual's role as a visible mediator dropped away in Stephenson's photographs as his focus shifted to empty landscapes. While photographing clouds, vast landscapes, oceanic horizon lines, icy Antarctic landscapes, and stars, and making photograms of plants, Stephenson became progressively more interested in capturing the transcendental power of the landscape. His style became simplified as his complex panoramas gave way to his direct transcriptions of the elements of stars, sky, sea, land, and plant life.

Although caught in real time, the more visually spare Stephenson's photographs become, the more they exist outside history, suspended in a moment of consciousness that is both of the moment and eternal. This stretching and slowing of time brings attention not only to our perception but often gives Stephenson's photographs a meditative quality that links the external world inexorably to an internal state of being.

Though people may be absent from Stephenson's more recent works, the human presence is made manifest in absentia. The more elemental and pristine the part of the natural world he depicts, the more it encourages us to consider the terms of our relationship to it. Nature may look remote and unchanging, but these days it is impossible for us to see the wilderness without also feeling its vulnerability to our influence. Global warming, pollution, mining, and other commercial land uses leave no part of the Earth untouched.

The human element is apparent in Stephenson's work in another, more subtle, way. In the early 1990s he began an extended series of photographs of the central oculus of European church domes and, around the same time, photographically charted the tracks of stars in the night sky. Despite their apparently disparate nature, these subjects are conceptually linked and, perhaps surprisingly, human-centered.

Both series explore the relationship between the individual and the infinite. They invite us to speculate on the eternal either by regarding the endless night sky or by gazing through a dome's focal point, which is considered the junction between Earth and heaven. Similarly, the "divine geometry" evident in both the traces of stars' movements and the intricately constructed and decorated church domes again make us consider the individual and our place in the cosmos.

In 2003 Stephenson extended his interest from the "eye" of the dome to the arched ceilings of the church vault. These equally transcendent photographs, which isolate another key aspect of traditional church architecture, are nonetheless of a different emotional order. Looking at these stone vaults is similar to lying beneath the hollow belly of a giant animal whose massive articulated stone spine "vertebrae" and sinewy "ribs" create an effect that is positively skeletal.

The anthropomorphic quality of these photographs is also reflected in the architectural language that describes their components: *groins*, *ribbing*, and *cells* are common terms suggesting the connection between the superstructure of the church and the human body. This corporeal link is made even more apparent in the juxtaposition of the photographs in which the twinned—almost panoramic—views appear to be attenuated spinal columns cast in stone. The cumulative effect suggests that the church is the symbolic body of humanity through which the divine is then worshipped.

Stephenson's project also charts the temporal and spatial evolution of ancient church vaults. Here we see a typology of vault forms: simple arched stone tunnels, or so-called barrel vaults, complex tierceron and lierne vaults with their added decorative ribs, and vast fan vaults constructed of intersecting conical shapes often covered with blind tracery motifs. The evolution of the Romanesque, and later Gothic styles, becomes clearly apparent, as do regional differences. Part of our pleasure in viewing these photographs comes from the seemingly infinite variety and complexity of forms and designs shown, and the contrast between the solidity of the stone and the delicacy of the stained glass windows through which pours illuminating sunlight.

However, to see this project as simply documentary is to miss the point. Certainly what Stephenson shows here transcribes various ecclesiastical ceilings, but the images also have an emotional resonance, which is their true purpose. The relentless upward view required of us is both awe inspiring and elevating: the sweep of the columns drawing the eye to the roofline has an intensely liberating sensation.

Taken as a group the experience becomes almost hallucinogenic. The cues for spatial depth drop away, and the dizzyingly upward perspective becomes fantastical as the heaviness of stone transforms into an airy lightness. These photographs oscillate between the abstract and the representational, the human and the divine, the personal and the impersonal, and they detail both the form and the feeling of spiritual spaces. In the process they invite us to consider life and its meaning. Indeed, the optical effect of these vaults has a spiritual lesson at its heart. By taking the viewers out of the mundane world of their personal burdens—if only temporarily—the experience of these vaults suggests contemplating the divine can offer respite from worldly problems.

If there is one persistent human characteristic, it is our need to know ourselves and to understand our place in the world. As Stephenson's beautiful photographs suggest, this desire has, perhaps, changed little since these great churches were built. To look upward to ponder our place within the cosmos is as natural an impulse now as it was for the early church builders, whose magnificent buildings are shown here. However, contained in that act of looking is a fascinating paradox. When we regard the multiplicity and grandness of these designs, it is as much an outward speculation as it is an inner movement of consciousness. And what we feel when we view these magnificent and sublime vaults leads us, ultimately and inexorably, toward a spiritual understanding of our inner self.

Dr. Isobel Crombie
Senior Curator, Photography, National Gallery of Victoria, Melbourne

Plates

PANTHEON
Rome, Italy, 117–38

BATHS OF DIOCLETIAN
Rome, Italy, 298–306,
remodeled from 1561 as Church of Santa Maria degli Angeli

Nave

BASILICA DI SAN MINIATO AL MONTE

Florence, Italy, 1013–62

Nave
MONREALE CATHEDRAL
Monreale, Italy, 1174–82

Crossing

MONREALE CATHEDRAL

Monreale, Italy, 1174–82

15

ST. MARK'S BASILICA
Venice, Italy, begun 1063

16

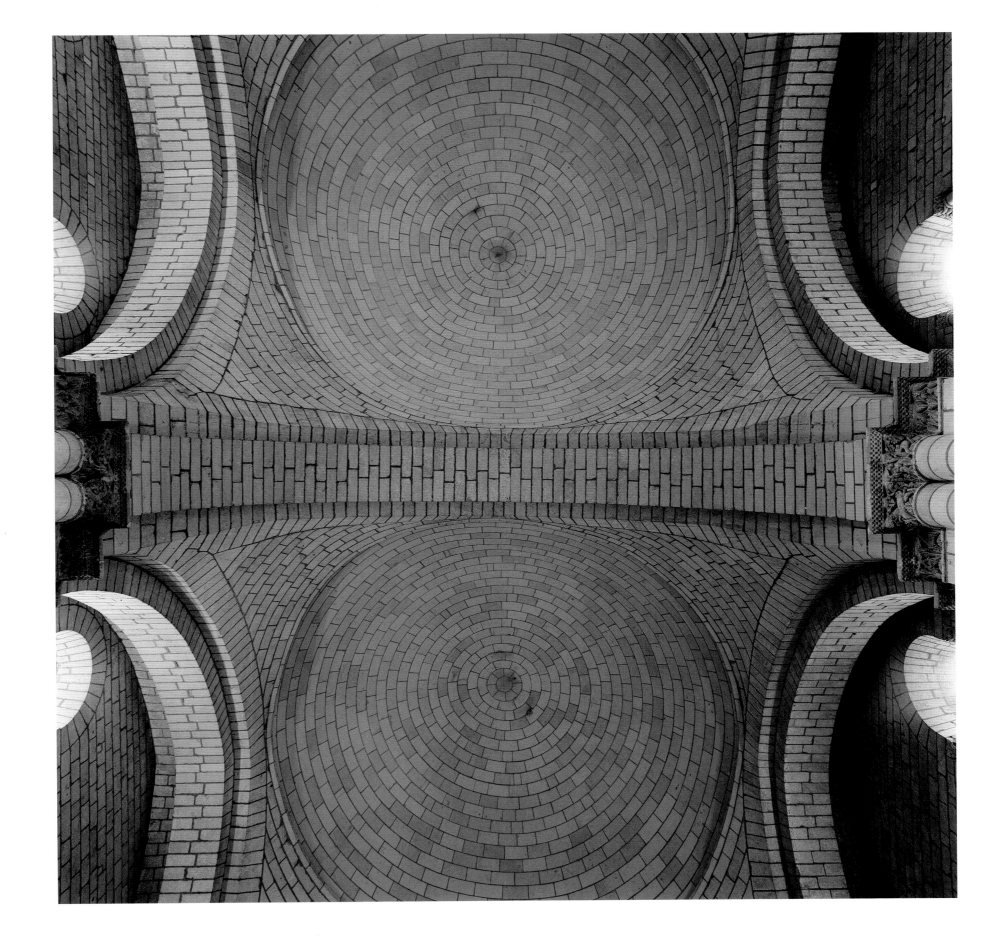

Nave
ABBEY OF FONTEVRAUD
Fontevraud, France, 1105–1119

Nave
ABBEY OF SAINT-FOY
Conques, France, 1050–1130

Nave
SAINT-SERNIN BASILICA
Toulouse, France, 1077–1120

Nave
Cathedral of St. James
Santiago de Compostela, Spain, 1075–1211

Nave
SPEYER CATHEDRAL
Speyer, Germany, begun 1030, vaults 1082–1137

Nave
CATHEDRAL OF ST. PETER
Worms, Germany, 1110–81, rib vault ca. 1171

Nave
Basilica of St. Mary Magdalene
Vézelay, France, 1096–1132

Nave
ABBEY OF FONTENAY
Fontenay, France, 1139–47

Nave

CHURCH OF SAINT ÉTIENNE, ABBAYE-AUX-HOMMES

Caen, France, 1070–81, vault 1120, rebuilt 1616

Crossing

CHURCH OF SAINT ÉTIENNE, ABBAYE-AUX-HOMMES

Caen, France, 1070–81, vault 1120, rebuilt 1616

27

Nave
LAON CATHEDRAL
Laon, France, 1160–1230

Crossing
LAON CATHEDRAL
Laon, France, 1160–1230, lantern tower ca. 1170–75

Choir
BASILICA OF SAINT-DENIS
Saint-Denis, France, 1140–44, modified 1231

Choir
BASILICA OF ST. MARY MAGDALENE
Vézelay, France, begun after 1165

31

Nave

CHURCH OF SAINT RÉMI

Reims, France, 1005–49, rebuilt and vaulted ca. 1150

Nave
WELLS CATHEDRAL
Wells, England, 1190–1230

33

Becket's Corona
CANTERBURY CATHEDRAL
Canterbury, England, 1175–84

Nave

Santa María de Santes Creus
Santes Creus, Spain, ca. 1174–1314

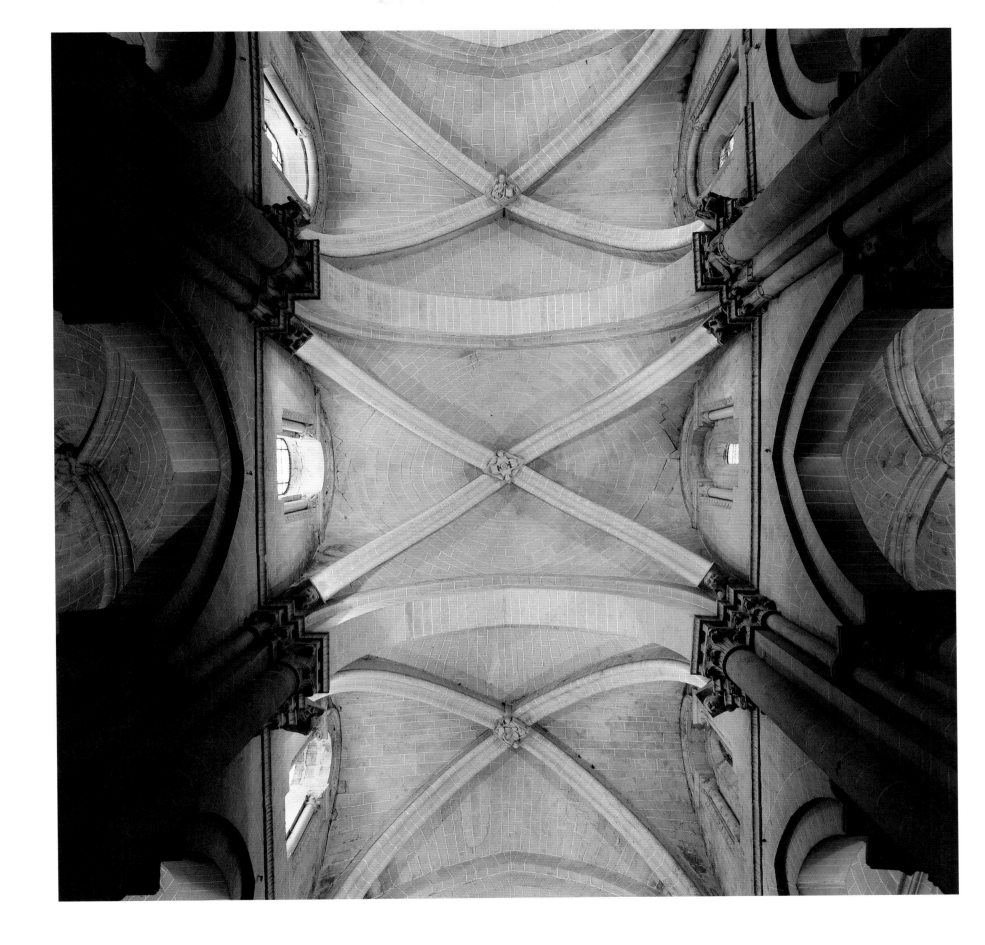

Nave
OLD CATHEDRAL
Salamanca, Spain, 1150–80

Nave
SANTA MARIA D'ALCOBAÇA
Alcobaça, Portugal, 1170–1223

Nave
CATHEDRAL OF NOTRE-DAME
Paris, France, 1163–1250

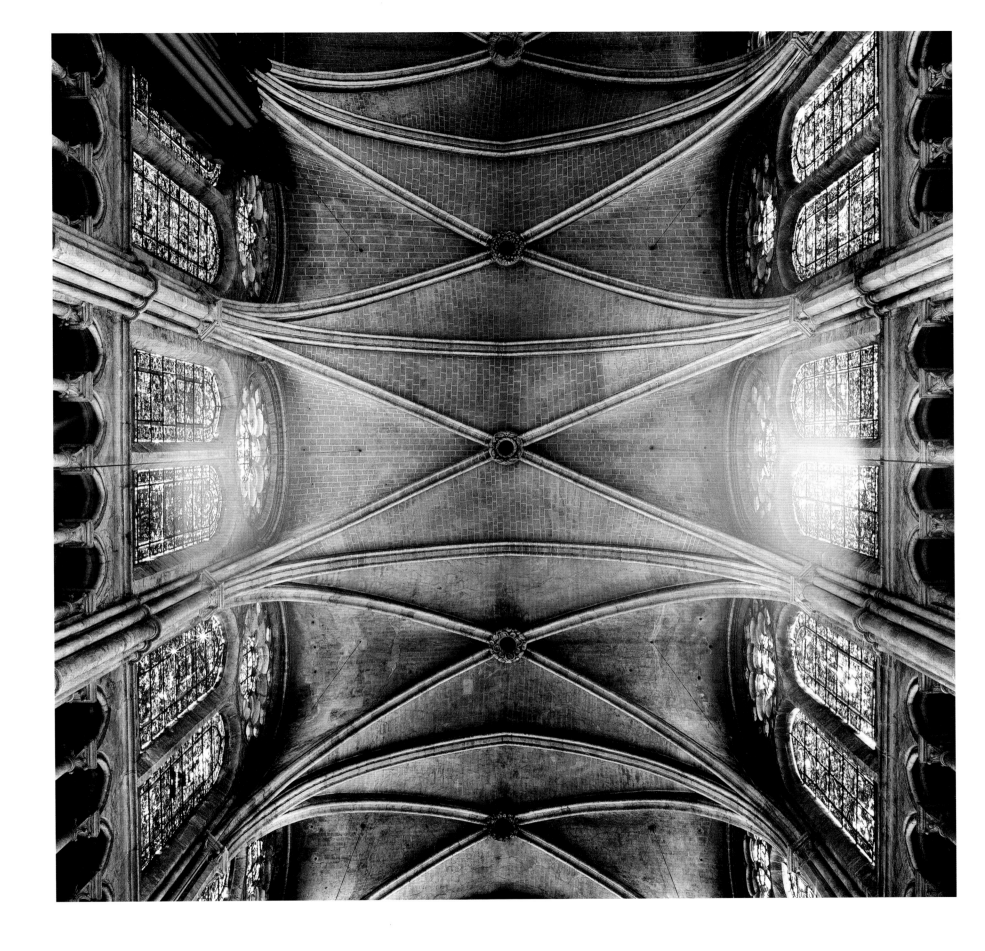

Nave

CHARTRES CATHEDRAL

Chartres, France, 1194–1260, vaults complete by 1217

Nave
Bourges Cathedral
Bourges, France, begun 1195, nave 1225–55

Nave
REIMS CATHEDRAL
Reims, France, 1211–85

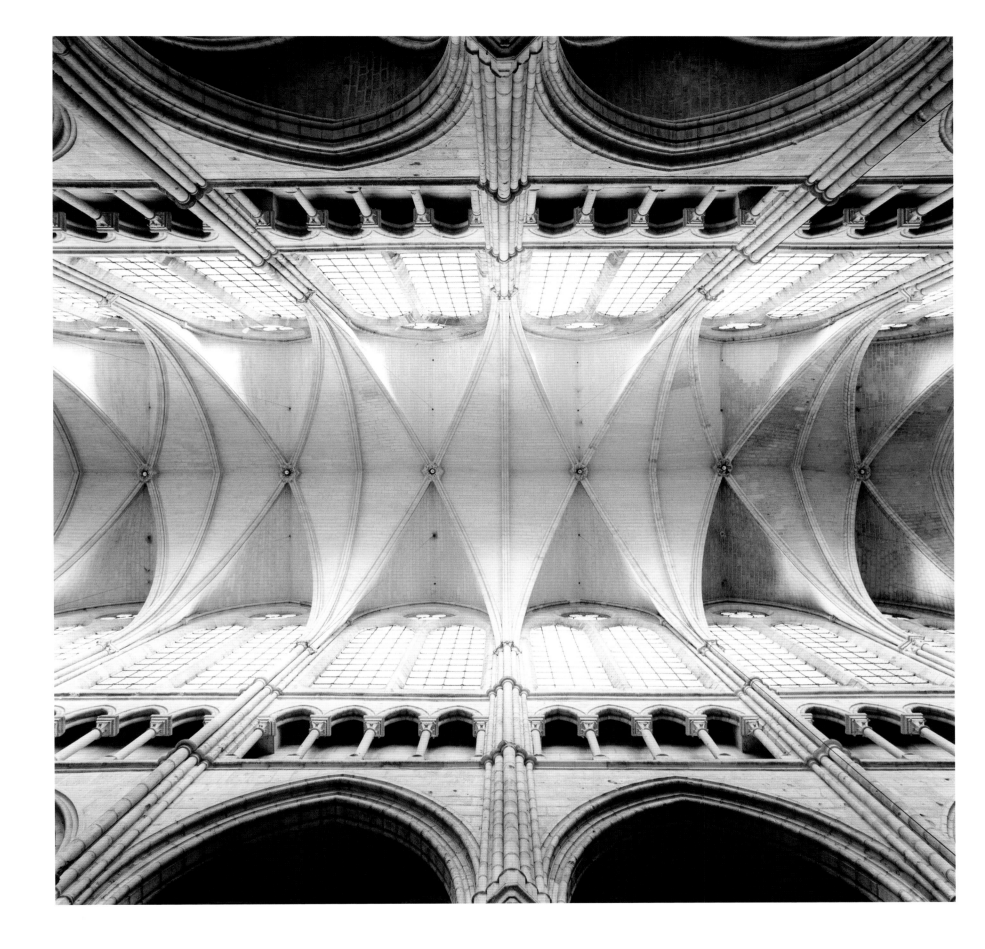

Nave

SOISSONS CATHEDRAL

Soissons, France, begun 1197

Crossing
Soissons Cathedral
Soissons, France, begun 1197

Choir
SOISSONS CATHEDRAL
Soissons, France, begun 1197

Nave
AMIENS CATHEDRAL
Amiens, France, 1220–36

Crossing
AMIENS CATHEDRAL
Amiens, France, completed 1269

Choir
AMIENS CATHEDRAL
Amiens, France, completed 1269

South transept arm
TROYES CATHEDRAL
Troyes, France, 1208–40

North transept arm
TROYES CATHEDRAL
Troyes, France, 1208–40

53

Choir
BEAUVAIS CATHEDRAL
Beauvais, France, 1225–1337

54

Choir
COLOGNE CATHEDRAL
Cologne, Germany, begun 1248

Nave
Sainte-Chappelle
Paris, France, 1242–48

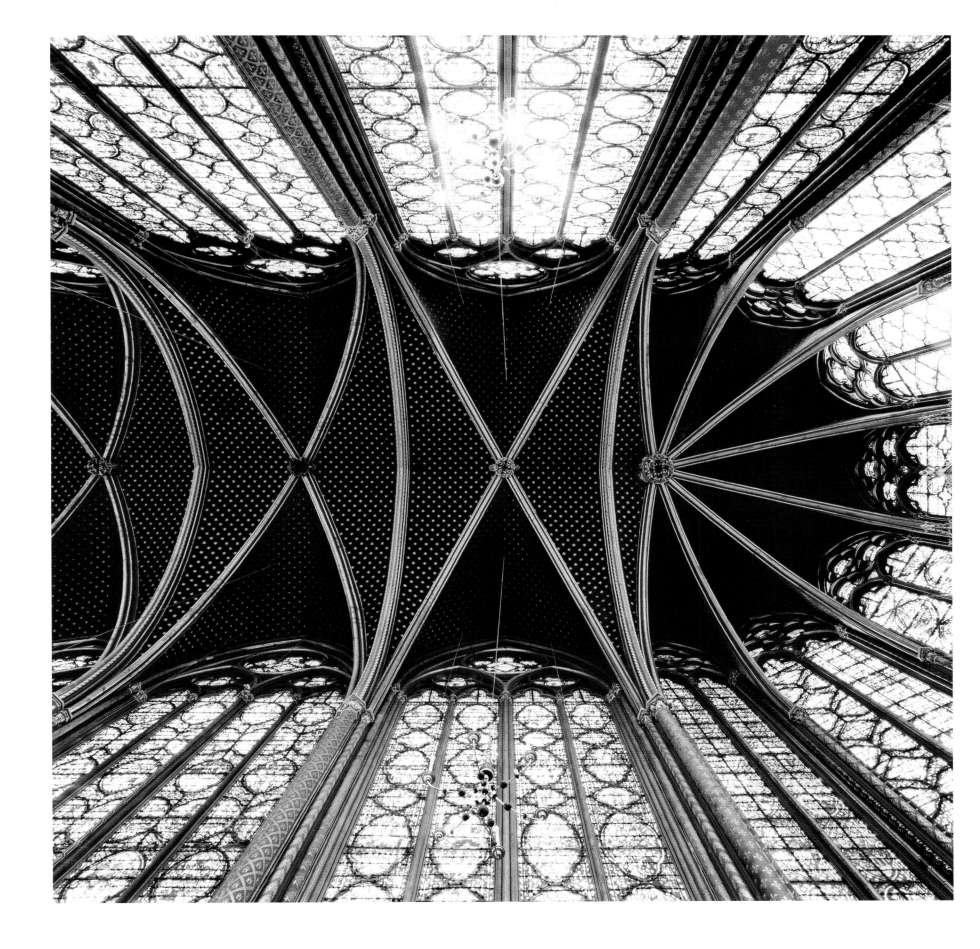

Choir
SAINTE-CHAPPELLE
Paris, France, 1242–48

Nave
BASILICA OF SAINT-URBAIN
Troyes, France, 1262–86

Choir
BASILICA OF SAINT-URBAIN
Troyes, France, 1262–86

59

Nave
SALISBURY CATHEDRAL
Salisbury, England, 1220–58

Choir
SALISBURY CATHEDRAL
Salisbury, England, 1220–58

61

Nave

WORCESTER CATHEDRAL

Worcester, England, ca. 1084–1396, vaults 1375–95

Choir
WORCESTER CATHEDRAL
Worcester, England, 1224–69

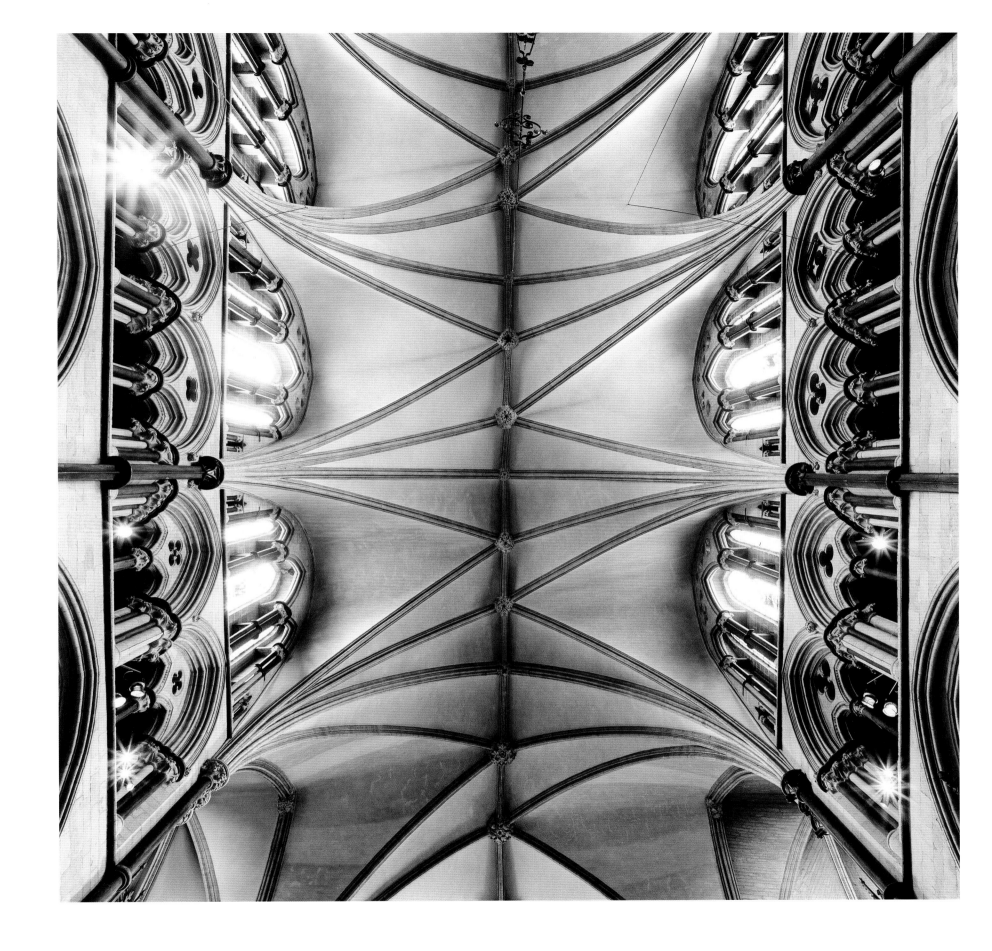

St. Hugh's Choir
LINCOLN CATHEDRAL
Lincoln, England, vault 1192–1200

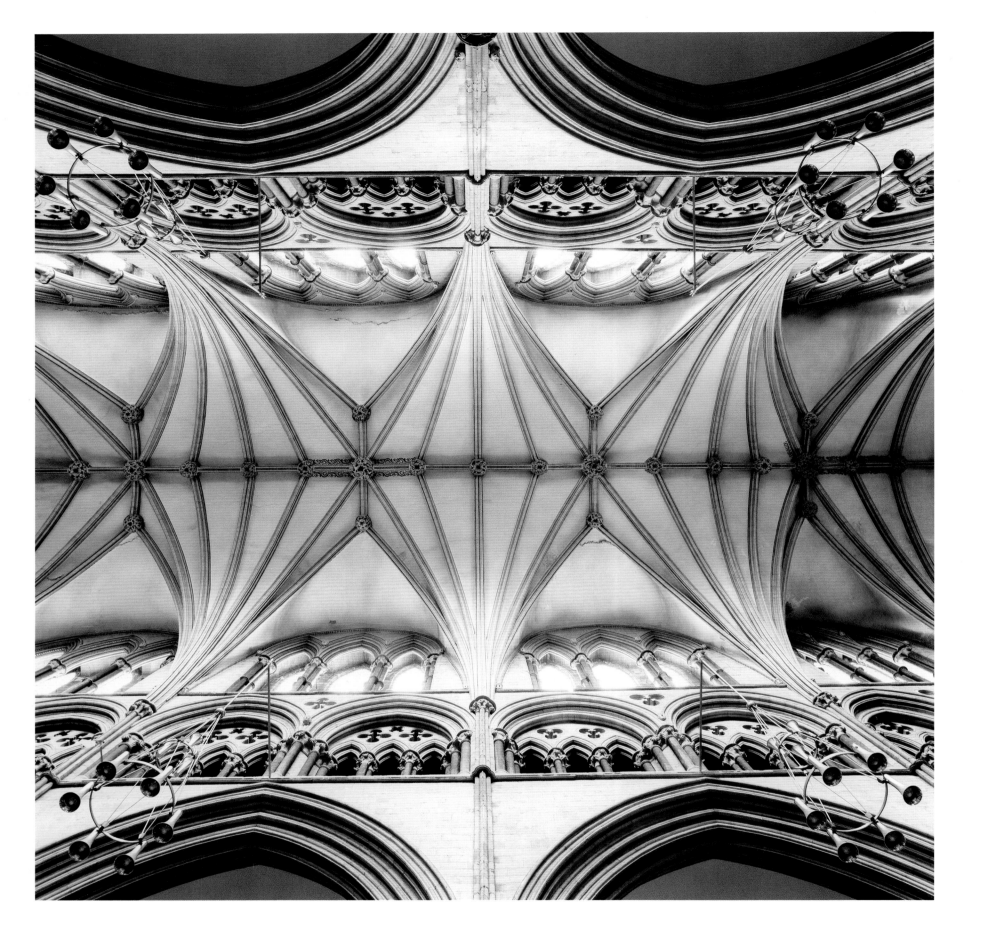

Nave
LINCOLN CATHEDRAL
Lincoln, England, 1225–53

Crossing

LINCOLN CATHEDRAL

Lincoln, England, 1238–1311

Angel Choir
LINCOLN CATHEDRAL
Lincoln, England, 1275–90

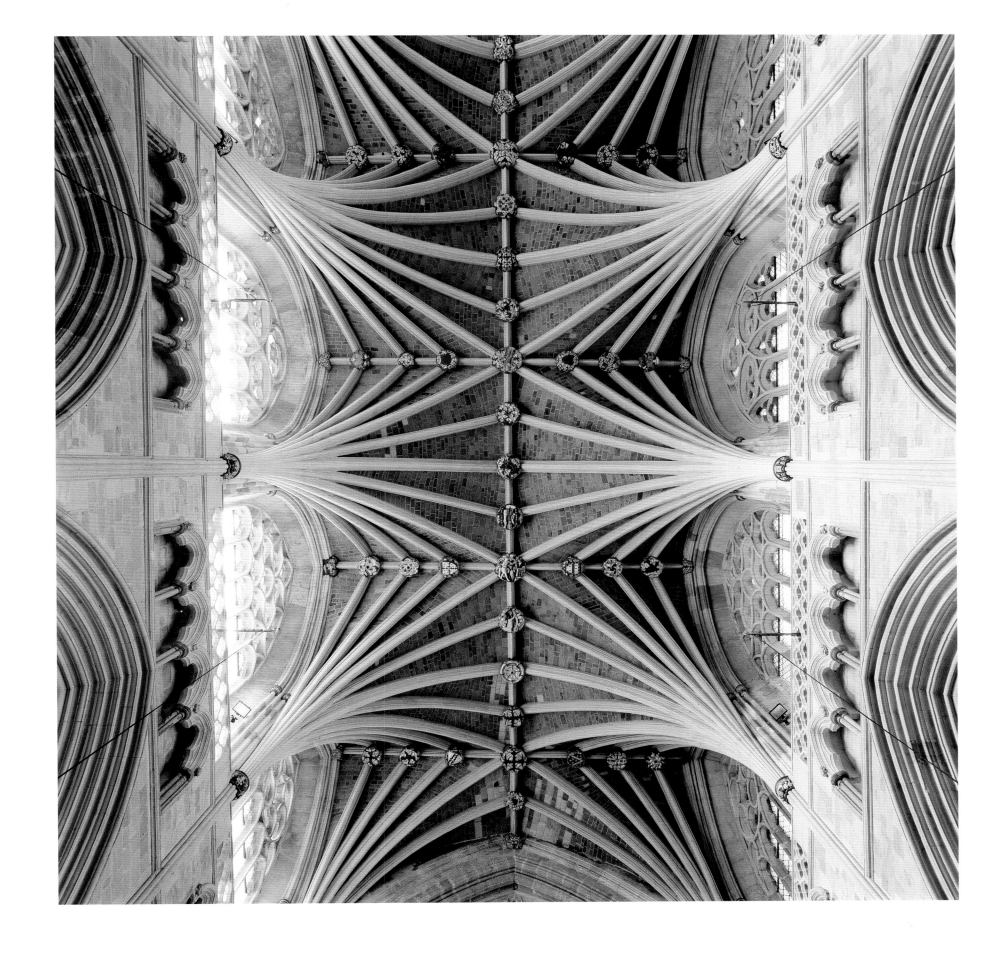

Nave

EXETER CATHEDRAL

Exeter, England, begun 1280, vaults 1353–69

Chapter House
LINCOLN CATHEDRAL
Lincoln, England, 1220–35

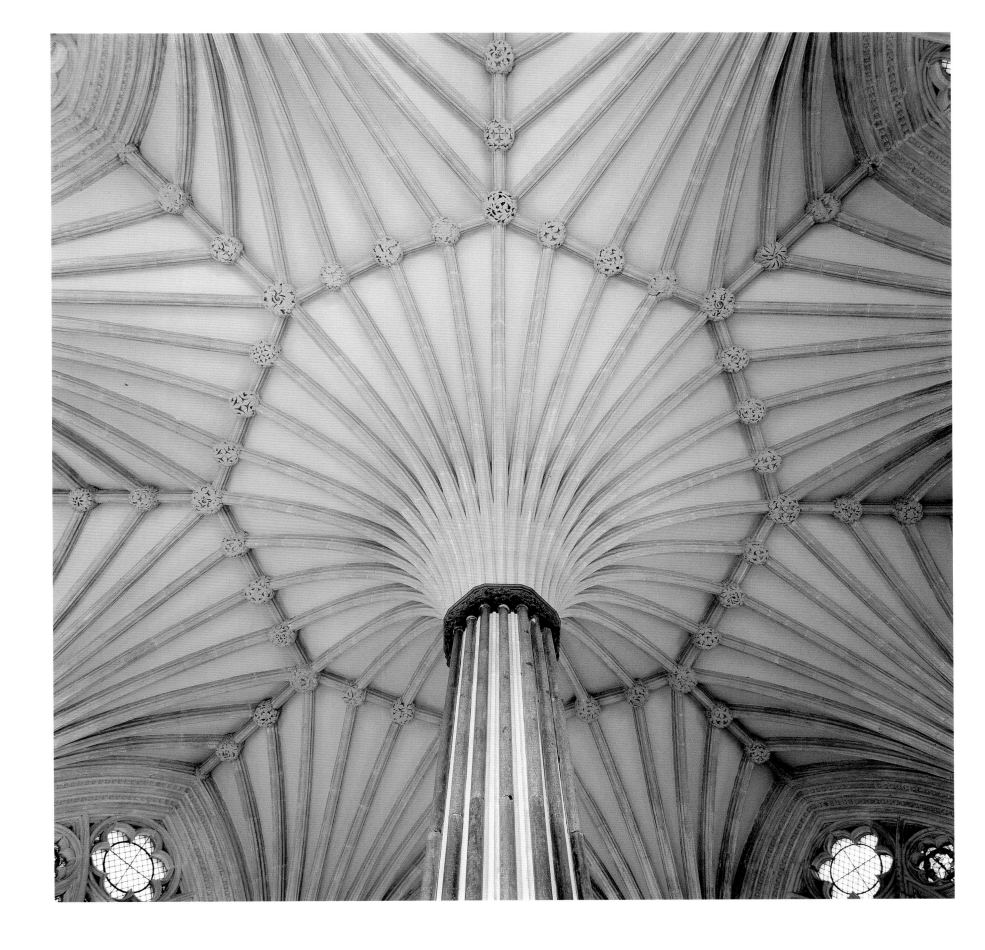

Chapter House
WELLS CATHEDRAL
Wells, England, 1298–1305

Nave
CHURCH OF THE JACOBINS
Toulouse, France, 1323–35

Choir
CHURCH OF THE JACOBINS
Toulouse, France, 1275–92

Nave
CATHEDRAL OF SAINTE-CÉCILE
Albi, France, 1282–1480

75

Nave
BASILICA OF SAN FRANCESCO D'ASSISI
Assisi, Italy, 1228–53

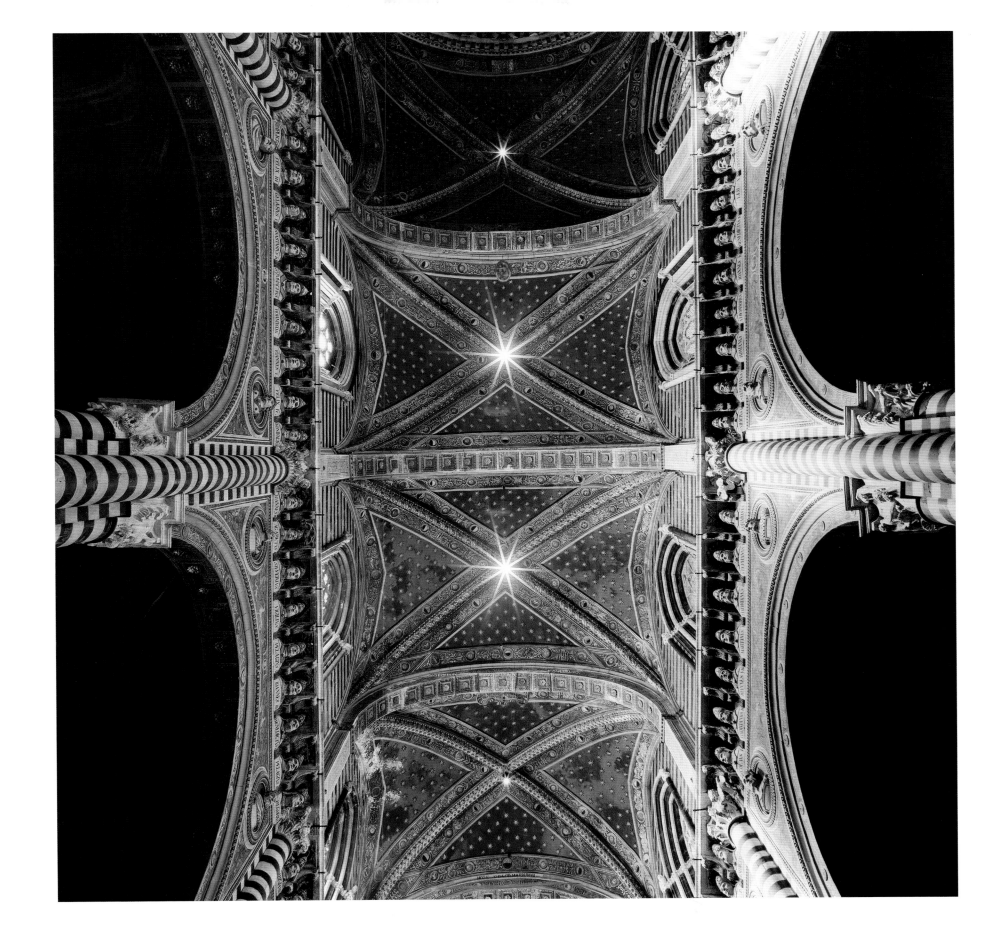

Nave
SIENA CATHEDRAL
Siena, Italy, ca. 1226–1370

Nave
ORVIETO CATHEDRAL
Orvieto, Italy, 1280–1368

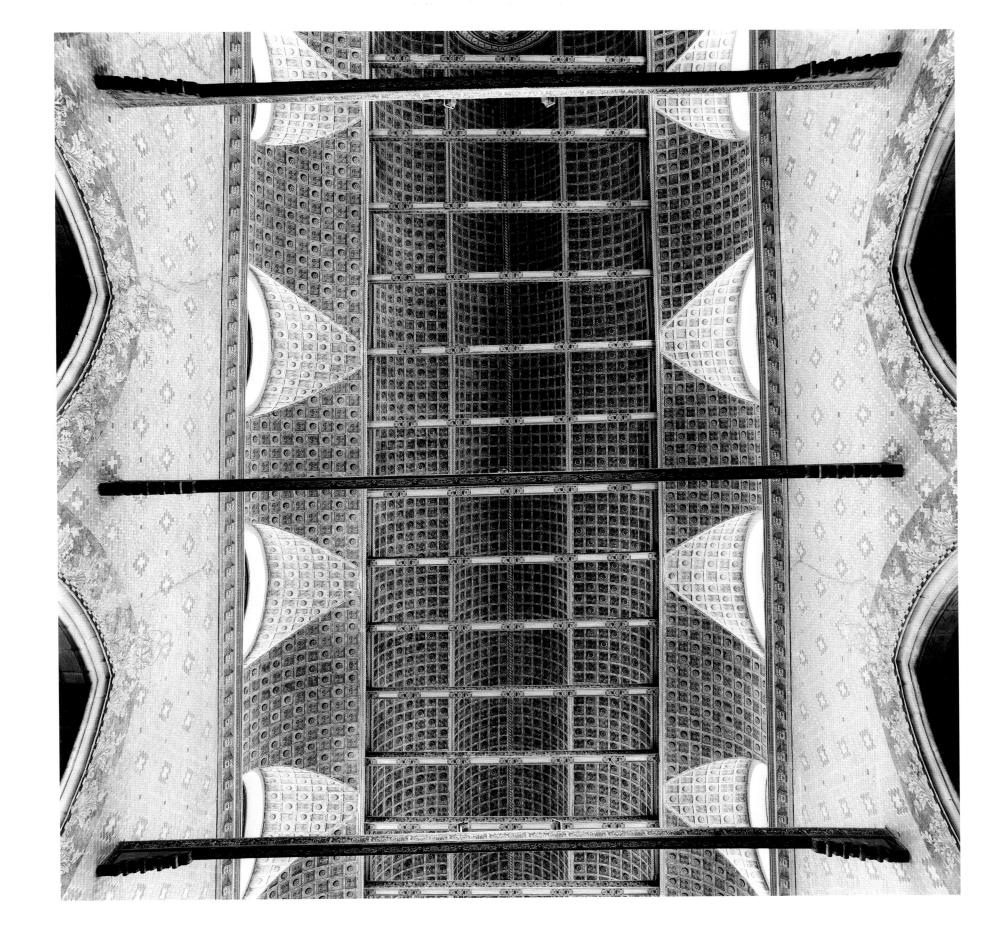

Nave
CHURCH OF SANTO STEFANO
Venice, Italy, 1325–74

Nave

Basilica dei Santi Giovanni e Paulo

Venice, Italy, 1333–1430

Choir

BASILICA DEI SANTI GIOVANNI E PAULO

Venice, Italy, 1333–1430

81

Nave
SANTA MARIA DEL MAR
Barcelona, Spain, 1329–83

Ambulatory
Santa Maria del Mar
Barcelona, Spain, 1329–83

83

Nave

St. Rombaut's Cathedral

Mechelen, Belgium, 1342

Nave
Saint Bavo's Cathedral
Ghent, Belgium, ca. 1200–1400

Nave

CATHEDRAL OF OUR LADY

Antwerp, Belgium, 1352–1531

Crossing
CATHEDRAL OF OUR LADY
Antwerp, Belgium, 1352–1531

Lady Chapel
WELLS CATHEDRAL
Wells, England, 1320–40

Crossing
PETERBOROUGH CATHEDRAL
Peterborough, England, 1325, rebuilt 1883–86

Chapter House
YORK MINSTER
York, England, ca. 1286–96

Lady Chapel
ELY CATHEDRAL
Ely, England, 1321–49

Octagon
ELY CATHEDRAL
Ely, England, 1322–46

Choir
WELLS CATHEDRAL
Wells, England, ca. 1329–45

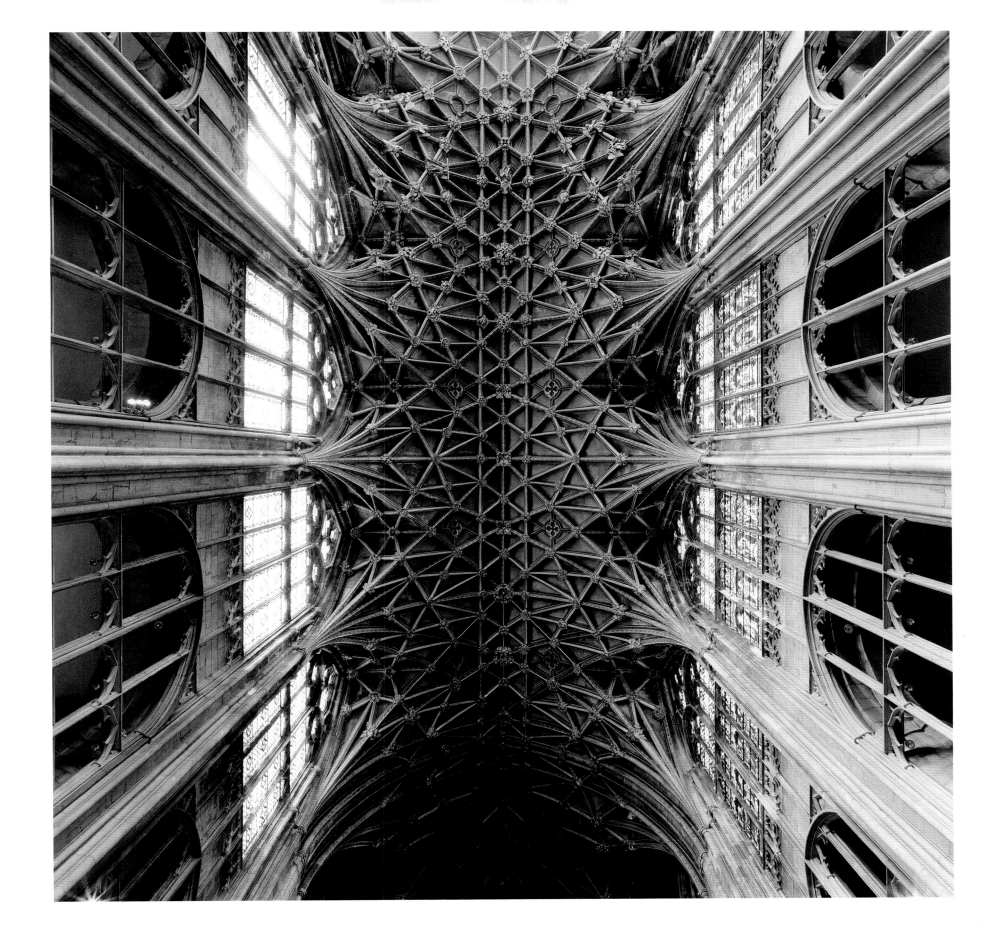

Choir
GLOUCESTER CATHEDRAL
Gloucester, England, 1337–67

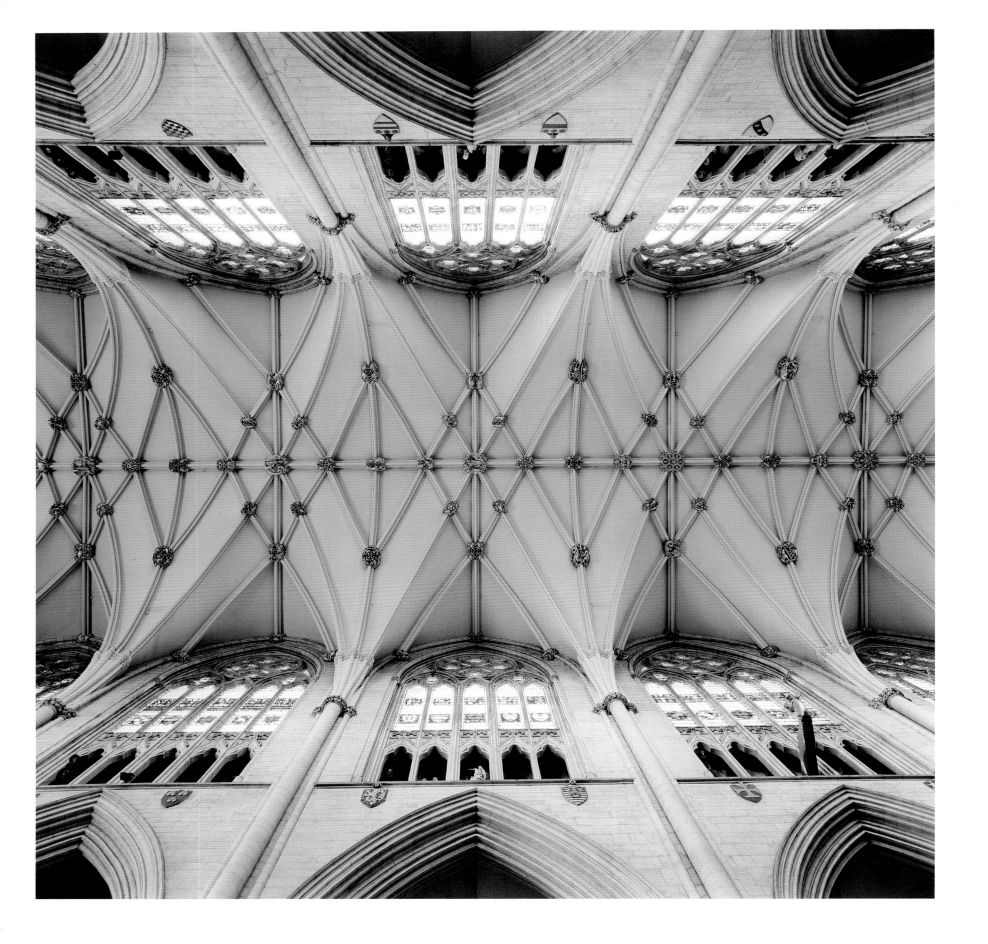

Nave

YORK MINSTER

York, England, 1292–1345, vault 1354–70

Crossing
YORK MINSTER
York, England, 1407–23, vault 1470–74

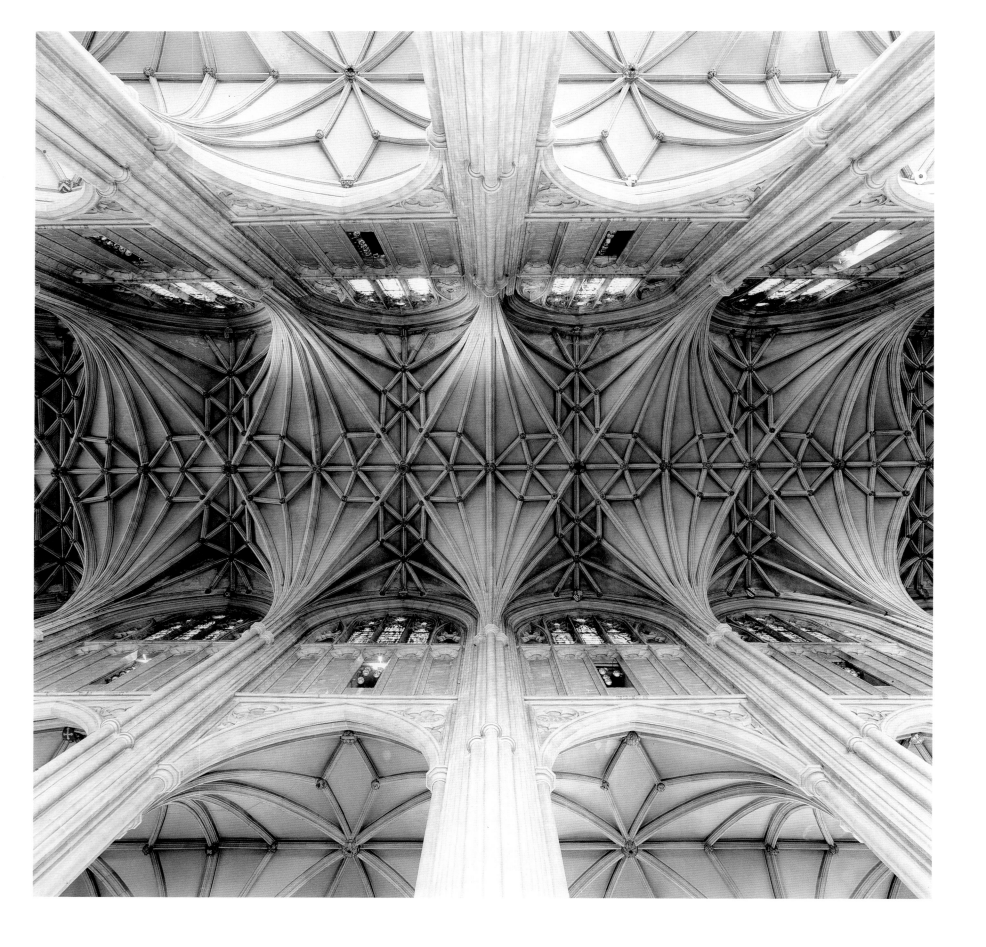

Nave
CANTERBURY CATHEDRAL
Canterbury, England, 1379–1405

Bell Harry Tower
CANTERBURY CATHEDRAL
Canterbury, England, 1493–1507

Nave
WINCHESTER CATHEDRAL
Winchester, England, 1394–1450

Crossing
WINCHESTER CATHEDRAL
Winchester, England, 1475–90

Nave
St. Mary's Church
Lübeck, Germany, 1277–1351

Choir
ST. MARY'S CHURCH
Lübeck, Germany, 1277–1351

103

Crossing
BAD DOBERAN MINSTER
Bad Doberan, Germany, 1294–1368

Choir
BAD DOBERAN MINSTER
Bad Doberan, Germany, 1294–1368

Nave
ST. VITUS CATHEDRAL
Prague, Czech Republic, 1344–1929

Crossing
St. Vitus Cathedral
Prague, Czech Republic, 1344–1929

Choir
CHURCH OF ST. SEBALDUS
Nuremberg, Germany, 1359–79

Choir
CHURCH OF THE HOLY SPIRIT
Landshut, Germany, 1407–61

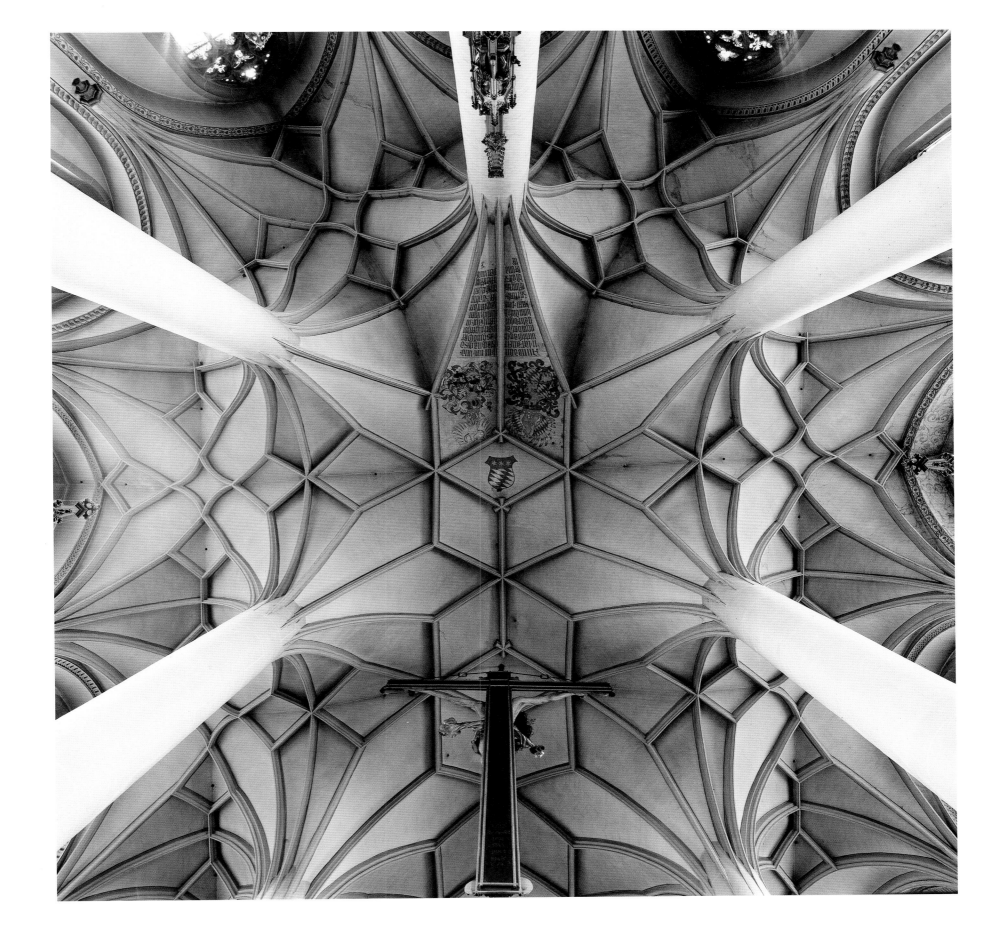

Choir
CHURCH OF ST. JOHN
Dingolfing, Germany, 1467–1502

111

Nave

CHURCH OF ST. MARTIN

Landshut, Germany, 1400–80

Choir
CHURCH OF ST. MARTIN
Landshut, Germany, 1385–1400

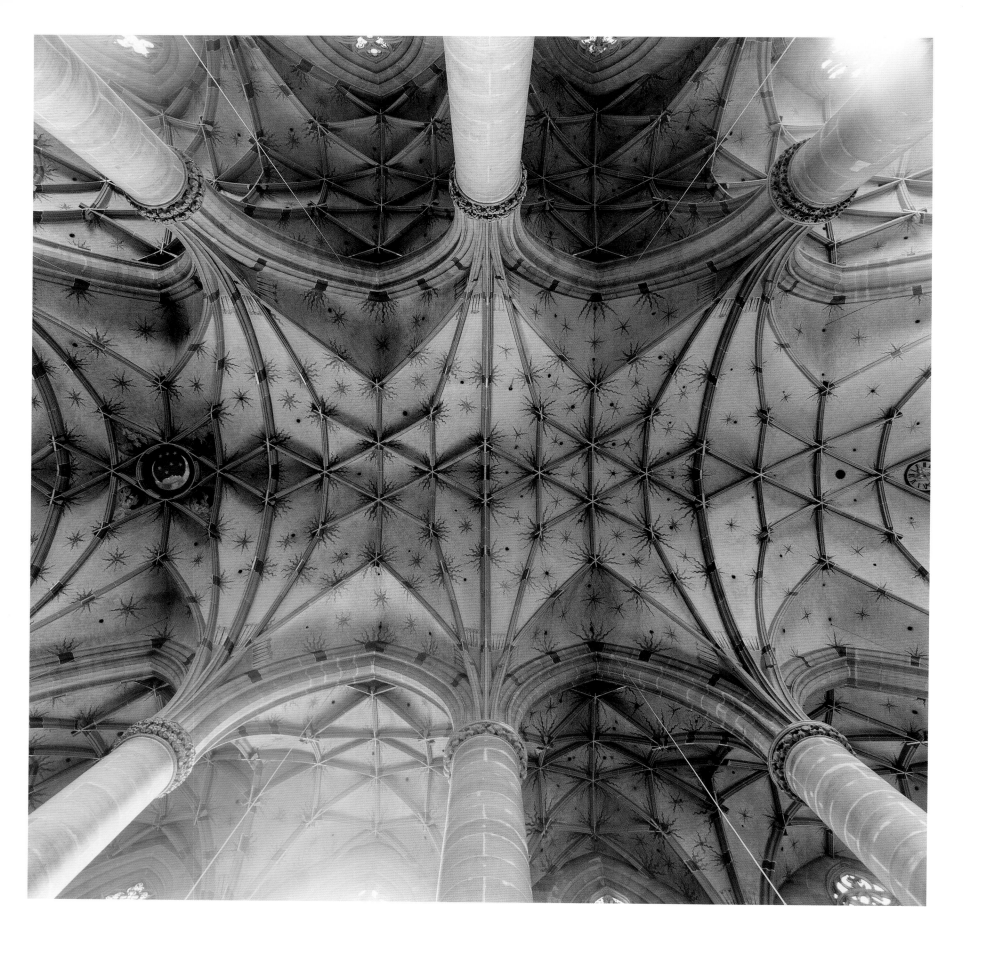

Nave
HOLY CROSS CATHEDRAL
Schwäbisch Gmünd, Germany, begun 1315, vaults 1497–1521

Choir

HOLY CROSS CATHEDRAL

Schwäbisch Gmünd, Germany, begun 1315, vaults 1497–1521

Nave
ST. STEPHEN'S CATHEDRAL
Vienna, Austria, begun 1359, vault 1467

Nave and choir
CHURCH OF ST. GEORGE
Dinkelsbühl, Germany, 1448–99

Nave
FRAUENKIRCHE
Munich, Germany, 1468–94

Nave
ST. MARY'S CHURCH
Pirna, Germany, 1502–46

Nave
ST. ANNE'S CHURCH
Annaberg-Buchholz, Germany, begun 1499, vault 1519–22

Nave

CATHEDRAL OF ST. BARBARA

Kutná Hora, Czech Republic, begun 1388, vault designed 1512 and built 1540–48

Choir
CATHEDRAL OF ST. BARBARA
Kutná Hora, Czech Republic, begun 1388

123

Nave
ST. MARY'S CHURCH
Stargard Szczeciński, Poland, 1292–1500

Choir
St. Mary's Church
Stargard Szczeciński, Poland, 1292–1500

125

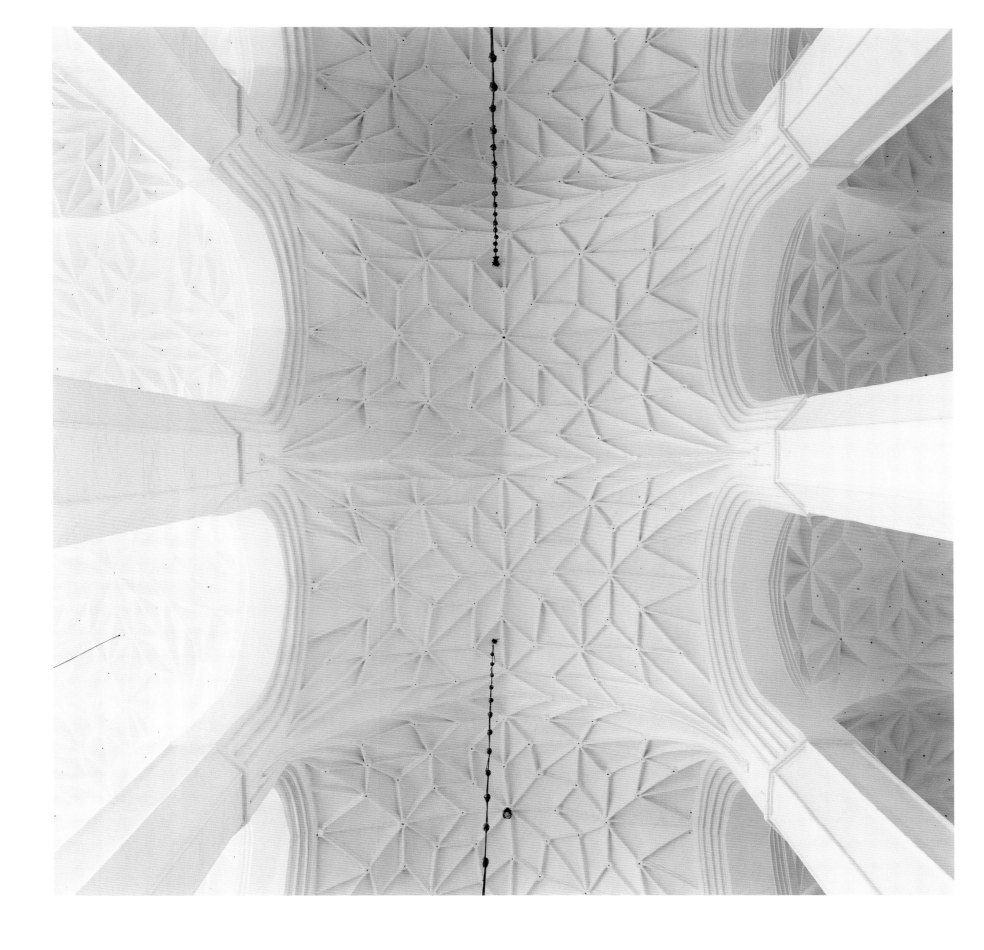

Nave

ST. MARY'S CHURCH

Gdańsk, Poland, begun 1379, vault 1496–1502

Choir

DEAN CHURCH OF LORD'S CONVERSION ON MOUNT TÁBOR

Tábor, Czech Republic, ca. 1480–1512

128

Choir
St. Bridget's Church
Gdańsk, Poland, ca. 1500

129

Choir
NORWICH CATHEDRAL
Norwich, England, begun 1096, vault 1472–99

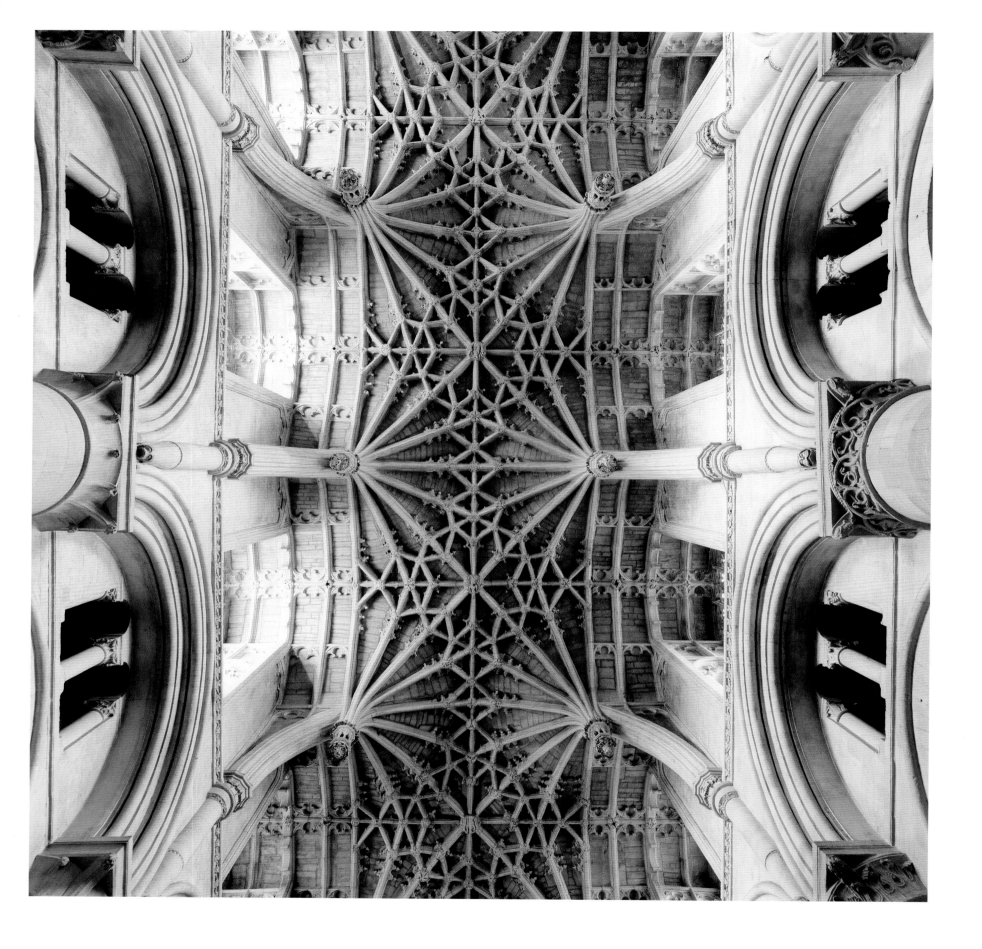

Choir

CHRIST CHURCH CATHEDRAL

Oxford, England, vault 1478–1503

132

Choir
KING'S COLLEGE CHAPEL
Cambridge, England, begun 1448, vault 1508–15

133

Nave
BATH ABBEY
Bath, England, 1501–39

Crossing
BATH ABBEY
Bath, England, 1501–39

Choir
SAINT-PIERRE CHURCH
Caen, France, 1528–45

Apse
SAINT-PIERRE CHURCH
Caen, France, 1528–45

137

Nave

SANTA MARIA DA VITÓRIA

Batalha, Portugal, begun 1388

Choir
SANTA MARIA DA VITÓRIA
Batalha, Portugal, begun 1388

Founder's Chapel
SANTA MARIA DA VITÓRIA
Batalha, Portugal, 1426–34

Unfinished Chapels
SANTA MARIA DA VITÓRIA
Batalha, Portugal, 1435–1533

Nave

CHURCH OF SANTA MARIA

Hieronymite Monastery, Belém, Portugal, 1501–17

143

Nave

MONASTERY OF SAN JUAN DE LOS REYES

Toledo, Spain, 1477–99

144

Crossing
Monastery of San Juan de los Reyes
Toledo, Spain, 1477–99

Choir

MONASTERY OF SANTA MARÍA DEL PARRAL

Segovia, Spain, 1455–75

Crossing

BURGOS CATHEDRAL

Burgos, Spain, 1466–1502, collapsed 1539, replaced 1569

Nave

CATHEDRAL OF SANTA MARIA

Seville, Spain, begun 1402, vault ca. 1515

Nave
PALENCIA CATHEDRAL
Palencia, Spain, begun 1321, vault 1514

Nave
NEW CATHEDRAL
Salamanca, Spain, 1512–38

Crossing
SEGOVIA CATHEDRAL
Segovia, Spain, 1522–1768

152

Choir
Segovia Cathedral
Segovia, Spain, 1563–91

153

Gothic Vaults
The Geometry of Transcendence

Introduction

To enter into a great Gothic church is to be instantly transported to another realm, seemingly beyond our earthly existence. Whatever our religious beliefs, the experience of awe is inescapable. Our eyes are led inexorably up the strong vertical lines of piers to the vaulted ceiling of the building, which seems to hover weightlessly like a great sail or bird above the diaphanous clerestory windows. It is impossible for us not to marvel at these transcendent structures, with their seemingly infinite design variations, or fail to be impressed by the ingenuity of the architects and builders who created the great medieval churches.

Over the course of five centuries, architects and builders developed an incredible vocabulary of Gothic vault forms for their churches, which stand today as the crowning achievement of stone building technology. From the domes, tunnel (or barrel), and groin vaults of Roman and Romanesque antecedents, the earliest Gothic rib vaults evolved in the twelfth century, revolutionizing vault construction. In the mature Gothic period of the thirteenth and fourteenth centuries, architects and builders experimented with numerous variations of vault design, and a final flowering of late Gothic architecture in the fifteenth and sixteenth centuries saw increasingly complex and decorative vault constructions. To understand how the Gothic vault developed and spread throughout Europe, it is helpful to take a look at medieval conventions of church construction.

By the eleventh century, church building in western Europe had evolved into a formal system of remarkable coherence and richness. The typical important church was constructed to a cruciform plan with four arms (see images on page 156): a longer nave to house the lay worshippers, intersected by two opposing and shorter transept arms, leading to a choir arm behind the main altar, which was generally reserved for the clergy or monks, and terminating in an east-facing apse of semicircular or polygonal design. Often, a circular dome or open, square crossing tower crowned the intersection of the four arms. Usually, the nave was built to the basilica scheme inherited from the early Christian period, in which a larger and higher central space, lit by clerestory windows, had lower side aisles flanking it, to allow visitors to circulate easily. In elevation, a middle story, or triforium, typically separated the clerestory from the side aisle arcades. In the French model, adopted frequently from the twelfth century on, aisles also flanked the choir arm, and a semicircular ambulatory running around the apse connected these aisles at the east end, often with radiating chapels.

Symmetry is fundamental to the design of the great churches. Of the multiple symmetries in church design, the most dominant (and most like that of our own bodies) is the bilateral symmetry along the length of the building. The components of the church's two sides typically mirror each other exactly. This symmetry is nowhere clearer than in a plan view, or its inverse, looking straight up at the center of a vault, where

TROYES CATHEDRAL *(see p. 52–53)*

the pattern formed by the ribs is arranged symmetrically around the spine of the ridge. These symmetries all serve to reinforce a sense of spiritual perfection and harmony.

Most churches were also built with proportions based on simple numeric ratios, either for practical or theological reasons. A square, with its four equal sides, could easily be divided in two to create the common bay proportions of 1:2. Similarly, a square rotated by 45° could be used to create an octagon: a form often used for crossing towers and chapels. Other numeric proportions that occur frequently relate directly to Christian symbolism, such as three, which refers to the Holy Trinity of the Father, the Son, and the Holy Ghost, or twelve, which symbolizes the number of apostles. The importance of particular numbers goes back to the Greeks—for the Pythagoreans, certain numbers were of mystical, transcendental significance, and the ratios of 1:2, 2:3, and 3:4 that underlie musical harmonics were of particular fascination to St. Augustine.

The standardized church form was certainly richly symbolic. The medieval church was the house of God, an evocation of the heavenly new Jerusalem, where God would dwell with the righteous. (Rev. 21, 22) The cruciform plan signified Christ's transcendence over death, and the cross was the sign he himself predicted would appear in heaven at the end of the world. (Matt. 24:30) Additionally, the modular bay system common to most Romanesque and Gothic churches, which evolved partly as an economical construction method, suggests the symbolism of infinity and eternity. Extending the length of the church by multiplying a seemingly indeterminate number of identical units powerfully evoked the vastness of the heavenly realm.[1]

The vaulted ceiling was a key part of this image of heaven. Although the earliest churches probably had flat wooden ceilings, by the Romanesque period the durability and fire resistance of the curved, masonry vaulted ceiling, along with its symbolism of eternity and heaven, made it a highly desirable addition to the basic church scheme. The symbolism of the ceiling—in particular of curved domical vaults—predates the Christian era. The circle, in having no beginning or end, is an extremely old and remarkably universal symbol of the concept of infinity, and by extension eternity, immortality, and heaven. The origins of the curved ceiling date to the earliest primitive dwellings of hides stretched over bent stick frameworks, and are an archetypal reminder of humankind's first dwellings.[2] In Roman times, it became common to cover mausoleums, temples, and other permanent structures with durable masonry vaults, and the domed Pantheon, one of the most extraordinary buildings in the world, still reminds us of this tradition. Spheres and their architectural derivations—arches, domes, and curved vaults—are thus closely linked symbolically to the overall conception of the church as the earthly evocation of heaven.

The great churches sometimes took centuries to build. Constructed of stone or brick masonry—an impressive and durable, but time-intensive and costly method—

they were enormous undertakings for the foundations that financed them. For example, Cologne Cathedral, begun in 1248, was not completed until late in the nineteenth century. The nave of St. Vitus Cathedral in Prague, begun in 1344, was not completed until the twentieth century—in both cases a period of more than five centuries elapsed, which is inconceivable in today's thinking. Due to the long construction times, with buildings often constructed in stages and then remodeled in successive campaigns, and the fact that written records are often sketchy, uncertainty surrounds the exact dates of the design and construction of many Romanesque and Gothic churches.

Many churches were, however, built in decades rather than centuries. In less than a hundred years, from 1180 to 1270, around eighty cathedrals were built in France alone, helping the spread of what has come to be known as Gothic architecture. A range of social and economic factors drove the church building boom of the Middle Ages. Most important among these were the resurgence of monasticism, and the increasing importance of towns as centers of exchange in the medieval agrarian economy. Both of these created the need as well as the funding for new churches—the vast expansion and growing wealth of the monastic orders resulted in the construction of new abbeys, and the increasing population and affluence of the towns led to the building of many important churches. Besides cathedrals, which by definition are the seat of a bishop (*cathedra* is Latin for bishop's throne), other churches considered in this book are monastic, collegiate, or parochial. Although kingly patronage was significant, and there are examples of one wealthy monarch funding a church, in general a wide range of additional outside sources raised income, including indulgences, collections, and votive gifts. Often a building committee, affiliated with but separate from the cathedral chapter, administered large projects.[3]

The role of the patron in the design process is not well established. Clearly, the church's liturgical needs were considered, but these were standardized and were applied flexibly in regard to their location within the church. The wishes of the patron were no doubt influenced by a sense of competition: the inclusion of features from other important churches, known either through proximity or fame, brought prestige to the new building—no bishop or king wished to build a church that was already outdone by an existing one. From this perspective, it is possible to view the developments in medieval church architecture as a process of borrowings or quotations from existing buildings, coupled with the degree of innovation required to solve the particular problems presented by the respective building.

The construction of a church or cathedral required the builders to have a complex mix of organizational skills, technical knowledge, and creativity. That architects' names were recorded during the Gothic period—for the first time since before the Dark Ages—is evidence that these skills were greatly admired. However, in most cases, particularly in the early Gothic period, the written record is poor or nonexistent, and the identity of the designers of many buildings is obscure. A master mason—a profession that we would understand as the architect today—coordinated building projects and oversaw all aspects of design and execution. Master masons did not have an academic training, but had generally risen up through the stonecutter ranks through demonstrated ability, learning empirically on the job, until they had shown the capacity to coordinate their own projects. Family connections were important, and as with most trades in the Middle Ages, the children of stonecutters often became stonecutters. The children of master masons were also more likely to become master masons themselves, as was the case with important architectural families such as the Parlers. Master mason Heinrich Parler, probably from Cologne, worked on the influential late-Gothic nave of the Holy Cross Cathedral at Schwäbisch Gmünd, Germany, for example. Other Parler family masons active at important buildings such as Ulm Minster and St. Vitus Cathedral during the late Gothic period include Peter (probably Heinrich's son), Heinrich II, Heinrich III, Michael I, Michael II, and Peter's sons Wenzel and Johannes. Peter Parler, who is renowned for his innovative work on the late Gothic cathedrals at Prague and Kutná Hora in Bohemia, became influential enough to be commemorated, along with archbishops and kings, by a carved portrait in the triforium at St. Vitus Cathedral in Prague.[4]

Masons were organized in workshops or lodges, where they initially apprenticed and learned the skills of their trade. There was some exchange of people and skills between the various lodges, and it was common for master masons to move around for their work, particularly once they had established a reputation with successful projects. This movement of masons was instrumental in the spread of Gothic architecture across Europe, and there is even evidence that master masons made special study trips to look at a particular building. The lodges also had a very important function as Gothic architecture developed and stonework became more standardized. Particularly in northern Europe, where construction had to stop during the winter months due to the freezing of mortar, work could continue in the heated workshop with the cutting of standardized components such as sections of ribs, using templates developed by the master mason. Full-scale master drawings were apparently also used to determine key design aspects, as some have been found scratched into building surfaces, such as floors. Few small-scale drawings have survived from the early period of Gothic architecture, but it seems likely that drawing would have been an important tool in communicating ideas to patrons, as were small-scale models. Certainly by the late Gothic period, architectural drawings and detailed plans became more commonplace.

Building a large church required a host of other workers and resources, besides the masons. Ground had to be leveled and cleared of any existing structures, and foundations dug: work that could be done by unskilled laborers. Stone had to be quarried, or a brick-works had to be established. A foundry needed to be in proximity, for the creation and repair of stonecutters' tools and other iron components, such as tie-rods and clamps. Most importantly, a supply of large timber, and skilled carpenters, along with a dedicated workshop, were essential to the construction of these mainly masonry structures.

Timber was used at all stages of construction, but can be grouped into three main requirements for temporary support. First, timber props or struts helped stabilize walls as they were built. Second, timber scaffolding was required, once the building rose above the ground level, for masons to access their work. Third, timber formwork, or centering, supported the masonry vaults until they were completed, the mortar had set, and they became self-supporting.

By its very nature formwork is a temporary structure and little detailed evidence has survived of how it was designed and used. Saws were uncommon in the early period and timber components were normally hand shaped by adze, making the cutting of struts and planks a time- and material-intensive procedure. The formwork thus presented a complex range of problems to the builders, as it needed to be strong enough to support the immense weight of the stone blocks that formed the vault, yet also had to be efficiently removed after the completed stone vault was self-supporting, so that the costly heavy timbers could be reused. Virtually nothing has remained in the written record of exactly how this was achieved, but modern research suggests that a system of opposing wedges was almost certainly used in the majority of cases, which could be knocked away to allow enough of a gap for the formwork to be partially dismantled and moved. Indeed this "decentering" was one of the most critical and dangerous stages of the entire building process, as this was the moment of truth when the actual strength of the masonry vault was first tested.

The small holes, which remain in the walls of medieval churches, provide evidence that many of these temporary timber supports did not reach all the way from ground level, except in the early stages of building. Rather, through the clever use of these holes as support points, which could later be plugged, scaffolds were moved up the walls. Ledges in the wall structure provided abutment points for formwork and props, allowing considerable economy of materials. Besides the temporary supports, timber was also used in the roof, which was still needed to protect the vaulted ceiling and make the building weather tight. In fact, once the walls were built, a roof might be completed next, which provided both a weatherproof work site and a structural platform from which to lift materials.[5]

The phases of construction varied from building to building, but most churches were constructed with the more liturgically important eastern choir section first, which allowed the building to be used before it was completed. The bay structure developed during the Romanesque period was a significant advantage, as the semicircular or polygonal eastern termination of the apse was structurally more stable, and adjacent bays could then be sequentially built moving westward, each deriving their stability from the abutting preceding one. The bay system, by its nature an agglomeration of near identical modules, also allowed significant economies in the time and materials required for the temporary timber work. As the building progressed from east to west, props, scaffolds, and centering could all be reused, often with little alteration. In fact, it is likely that particularly with the regular tunnel-vaulted buildings, such as the major Romanesque pilgrimage churches—the Abbey of Saint-Foy (Conques, France), Saint-Sernin Basilica (Toulouse, France), and the Cathedral of St. James (Santiago de Compostela, Spain)—large rolling structures similar to siege engines were used for the formwork of each vaulted bay. The use of these and other techniques dates back at least to the Romans, who built massive, complex masonry structures, from aqueducts to buildings.

The Origins of the Gothic Vault (100–1190)
From Roman to Romanesque: Domes, Tunnel, and Groin vaults

The medieval builders could look back at the impressive vaults of remaining Roman structures and draw inspiration and insight from them. The Romans had developed an architectural vocabulary of forms derived from the circle, including arches, domes, and tunnel and groin vaults, that allowed them to construct highly durable masonry structures, many of which are still standing today. However, much of the Romans' building knowledge was lost in the early Christian era and had to be reinvented by the Romanesque and Gothic builders. Sometimes it was not rediscovered until modern times—a most obvious example of this is the secret of hydraulic mortars, which the Romans discovered by combining volcanic ash, lime, and water. Hydraulic mortar, as opposed to the simple lime mortars the medieval builders used, does not need to dry but sets through chemically combining with water. Of far greater strength than lime and sand mortars, it could either bed masonry blocks, or, in combination with a rubble aggregate, make concrete, a material utilized for one of the greatest structures left by the Romans.[6] The PANTHEON (117–38), built by Emperor Hadrian, is a monolithic concrete dome spanning 142 feet (43 meters), a scale unmatched in any building until the construction of the dome on the Basilica di Santa Maria del Fiore (Florence, Italy) well over a thousand years later. The dome is built of Roman pozzolana concrete, using aggregates of volcanic tufa rock to reduce weight and thrust on the massive load-bearing walls of the supporting cylindrical drum. The interior surface is a latticework of coffered recesses, further reducing weight while retaining a gridlike reinforcing structure slightly reminiscent of later Gothic vaults.[7]

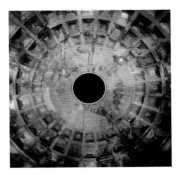

PANTHEON (*see p. 11*)

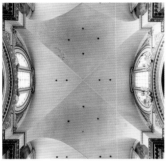

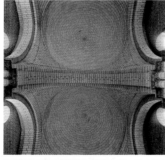

In addition to their early use of unreinforced concrete as a construction method, the Romans were also master builders of monumental masonry arches and vaults of various types using massive cut stone blocks. Roman skill in arch construction can still be seen in the numerous remaining Roman aqueducts supported by multiple tiers of huge stone semicircular arches. The simplest Roman vault was the tunnel vault (also called barrel vault), which, like an arch extended longitudinally, is semicircular in cross section. A key problem of the tunnel vault is the immense spreading lateral force, which the weight of the masonry directs onto the supporting walls—like an arch, the tunnel vault is only stable as long as this spreading thrust can be contained by massive supporting walls and piers.

Roman basilicas and baths also employed groin vaults, which result from two intersecting tunnel vaults. The Romans were the first to exploit this vault type, which has an advantage of reducing the immense spreading force on the walls of the simple tunnel vault, and also facilitating high windows at the transverse terminations of the vault. An example can still be seen at the Baths of Diocletian (298–306) in Rome, which Pope Pius IV commissioned Michaelangelo to renovate in 1561 as the Church of Santa Maria degli Angeli.[8] Here each of the three rectangular groin vaults spans 56 feet (17 meters) and rises 74 feet (22.5 meters) above the floor.[9] The outward thrust of the groin vaults is resisted by massive lateral walls, which provide no obstruction to the lighting from the generous clerestory windows allowed by the groin vaults.

Groin vault construction fell into relative obscurity after the fall of the Roman Empire, until Carolingian and Romanesque builders started to employ them in their stone buildings. Although much Roman building technology was lost, medieval builders continued to look to Rome for its vocabulary of classic architectural forms. The dome, for example, remained a highly significant vault form throughout the successive phases of Christian architecture.[10] Massive domes were used in many Byzantine and Romanesque churches. One of the most compelling examples is that of St. Mark's Basilica (begun 1063) in Venice, with its Greek cross plan and five domes, which, like all the interior surfaces of St. Mark's Basilica, are sheathed in a glittering mosaic skin of gold. The domes are supported on massive arches, which are like short tunnel vaults linking the domed spaces. The enormous domed church of Hagia Sophia (537) in Constantinople influenced a host of copies throughout the Christian world, and was a key model for St. Mark's Basilica as well as the domed churches of the Aquitaine region in France. Though sometimes these had a Greek cross plan like St. Mark's Basilica, they could also take the curious form of a long nave with a succession of domed bays, as can be seen in the Abbey of Fontevraud (1105–19).[11]

Besides the dome, Romanesque architecture made extensive use of flat wooden ceilings, either as permanent solutions or temporary measures that were later replaced by

Cross section of tunnel vault
Baths of Diocletian (*see p. 12*)
St. Mark's Basilica (*see p. 16*)
Abbey of Fontevraud (*see p. 17*)
Basilica di San Miniato al Monte (*see p. 13*)

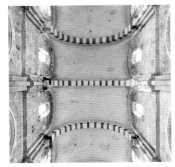

MONREALE CATHEDRAL (*see p. 14*)
CATHEDRAL OF ST. JAMES (*see p. 21*)
SAINT-SERNIN BASILICA (*see p. 19*)
ABBEY OF SAINT-FOY (*see p. 18*)
BASILICA OF ST. MARY MAGDALENE (*see p. 24*)

masonry tunnel or groin vaults. Some of the most beautiful examples of these wooden roofed churches remain in Italy, for example the exquisite BASILICA DI SAN MINIATO AL MONTE (1013–62) in Florence.[12] Here a painted wooden ceiling with exposed beams and rafters surmounts walls faced with polished marble in a decorative black-and-white pattern. At the Norman-Byzantine MONREALE CATHEDRAL (1174–82) in Sicily, the decorative effect is taken even further by gilding the exposed timber roof members of the nave and crossing, continuing the golden motif of the mosaic wall surfaces.[13] The walls of both Basilica di San Miniato al Monte and Monreale Cathedral are characteristic of one version of the Italian Romanesque—their surfaces are flat and continuous, with large expanses of decoration uninterrupted by vertical bay divisions. This is quite different than the defined bay divisions of the large, tunnel-vaulted Romanesque pilgrimage churches found in France and Spain.

THE ROAD TO SANTIAGO AND THE PILGRIMAGE CHURCHES

One of the most important pilgrimage routes during medieval times was the Way of St. James. The many thousands of pilgrims that walked the long road to Santiago de Compostela in northwestern Spain, to visit the tomb of the apostle St. James, are evidence of medieval piety, and an expression of the cult of relics, and indeed, death, that permeated early Christianity. The majority of people in the Middle Ages saw death as a short-term transition between this life and the next—either heaven or hell. Churches built to house important relics, such as the CATHEDRAL OF ST. JAMES (1075–1211) in Santiago de Compostela, became destinations for the faithful, where they could improve their chances for heaven. The Cathedral of St. James is a key example of a widespread pilgrimage church type, which included other great churches in France along the major pilgrimage roads such as SAINT-SERNIN BASILICA (1077–1120) at Toulouse and the ABBEY OF SAINT-FOY (ca. 1050–1130) at Conques. These churches all have a long nave with aisles and a gallery, a large transept with a crossing tower, and are tunnel-vaulted the length of the nave at a uniform height, which in the case of the Cathedral of St. James is 68 feet (20.7 meters). Rectangular piers with attached shafts lead to heavy transverse arches, which define regular rectangular bays.[14]

A related design is found in France at the BASILICA OF ST. MARY MAGDALENE (1096–1132) in Vézelay built at the start of an important pilgrimage road to Santiago de Compostela. The walls of the Basilica of St. Mary Magdalene are much flatter, however, and more continuous than those at Santiago, Conques, or Toulouse, with rectangular bays that are groin- rather than tunnel-vaulted. The slightly curving lines of the groins in the Basilica of St. Mary Magdalene demonstrate the difficulties that Romanesque builders faced in constructing straight groin vaults, particularly over rectangular bays. Creating a simple curved groin line that looked straight was a

SPEYER CATHEDRAL (*see p. 22*)
CATHEDRAL OF ST. PETER (*see p. 23*)

significant technical and aesthetic problem for the medieval builder, and is probably one of the factors that led to the development of the ribbed groin vault in the early Gothic period.[15]

Two enormous Romanesque churches somewhat related to the Vézelay type are found along the Rhine in Germany. The imperial SPEYER CATHEDRAL (1030–61) and the CATHEDRAL OF ST. PETER (1110–81) in Worms, are both large by Romanesque standards—the height of the nave vaults in Speyer Cathedral is 102 feet (31 meters).[16] Like at Vézelay, the walls are much flatter and more continuous, because, although there are aisles linked by low arcades, there is no gallery, but instead a low clerestory. Though the piers still have attached shafts leading to transverse arches, the bays are square rather than rectangular and are covered with groin vaults. Speyer Cathedral's groin vault dates from 1082–1137, and the Cathedral of St. Peter at Worms has a later ribbed vault from about 1171.[17]

MONASTICISM AND THE POINTED ARCH

The high degree of medieval piety demonstrated by the pilgrimages of the Middle Ages also drove the rapid growth of monasticism, with a resulting increase in church building activity. Medieval society was divided by three essential ranks—clergy, knights, and laborers—defined by their key occupations of prayer/teaching, fighting/defense, and work/farming. Monks were originally not ordained and existed somewhere in between the clergy and the laymen, having a special role within the religious orders; their sequestered way of life was seen as an example to others of spiritual commitment. Monks often came from a background of privilege and property, and acceptance into a medieval monastery was usually dependent on two conditions being met: spiritual suitability, as well as a gift, often land. Through this means the monasteries acquired enormous wealth during the Middle Ages. By the eleventh century, the monastery founded at Cluny, France in 910 by William of Aquitaine had become one of the most important monastic centers in Christendom—at the height of its powers it controlled a Benedictine family of more than one thousand monasteries.[18]

The enormous third church built at the Abbey of Cluny (1088–1121)—now mostly destroyed—was planned as one of the largest and most lavish in western Europe, with a height of 97 feet (29.5 meters) in the nave.[19] Its high pointed vault was a solution to the long-standing problem of building a tunnel vault over clerestories. Semicircular tunnel vaults created an immense amount of lateral thrust, pushing the tops of the supporting walls apart. The steeper sides of the pointed "Burgundian" vault in the Abbey of Cluny had a reduced component of lateral thrust compared to a semicircular tunnel vault, and could be more easily contained within the high walls required to accommodate a substantial clerestory.

CROSS SECTION OF POINTED TUNNEL VAULT

ABBEY OF FONTENAY (*see p. 25*)

An early example of a pointed tunnel vault can still be seen at the Cistercian monastery church of the ABBEY OF FONTENAY (1139–47). Like the Cluniacs, the Cistercians were a monastic set with a highly centralized organizational structure, founded at Saint-Nicolas-lès-Cîteaux, France in 1098 by Robert of Molesme.[20] In contrast to the Abbey of Cluny's extravagance, the austerity of the Cistercian ethos is echoed in their architecture. The Abbey of Fontenay has no clerestory; instead, windows at the ends and the crossing provide the only light for the nave. The long tunnel vault is pointed in profile, and pointed transverse arches, rectangular in profile, spring from attached shafts to separate the bays. The arcade's pointed arches echo this simple arrangement. Compared with the profile of the groin vault at the Basilica of St. Mary Magdalene in Vézelay, the tunnel vault at the Abbey of Fontenay rises much more steeply to its apex—an aspect that was to be crucial to the development of Gothic vaults. The Cistercians built monasteries all over Europe during the next few centuries and are credited with a significant role in the spread of the Gothic style.

NORMAN ARCHITECTURE AND THE FIRST RIB VAULTS

After the pointed vault, the second key element in the development of the Gothic vault was applying carefully cut stone ribs to groin vaults, which arose in Norman Romanesque churches during the eleventh and twelfth centuries. After the Normans had settled in northern France around 911 and converted to Christianity, they built a significant number of churches both in Normandy and in England (after the Norman Conquest in 1066). Many of the Norman churches were attached to abbeys, such as the CHURCH OF SAINT ÉTIENNE (at the former Abbaye-aux-Hommes, 1066), established at Caen by William the Conqueror. The Church of Saint Étienne is indicative of the consistent style of the Norman Romanesque at this time, characterized by bays strongly defined by the vertical divisions of compound shafted piers, which—like those of the pilgrimage churches—continue as semicircular transverse arches across the vault. The length of a bay is half its width, a proportion that had become fairly standard by this time. Semicircular arches are also used longitudinally in the arcades, lending homogeneity to the whole interior, which includes a substantial middle story of galleries almost as tall as the arcades. This creates a characteristic Norman Romanesque "thick wall" effect emphasized by the recession and spatial depth behind the interior wall. Like the pilgrimage churches, the Church of Saint Étienne has a lantern tower above the crossing.

CHURCH OF SAINT ETIENNE (*see p. 27*)
CHURCH OF SAINT ETIENNE (*see p. 26*)

Rather than the tunnel vaulting of the pilgrimage churches, Norman architects favored the groin vaults of the Roman type, a factor that was a necessary prerequisite for the acceptance of ribbed vaults. The first ribbed groin vaults probably occur in the side aisles (1093–95) at Durham Cathedral in England. This was quickly followed by the

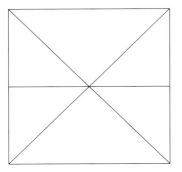

occurrence of ribbed vaults in other parts of Europe during the twelfth century. The present vault at the Church of Saint Étienne was rebuilt in 1616, presumably as a copy of the original rib vault (ca. 1120–35).[21] The transverse arches are reduced to relatively thin ribs, which are echoed by diagonal ribs of a similar dimension that spring from alternate piers and cross in the center of each alternate bay. This creates roughly square sexpartite vaults across double bays, each divided into six sections by the diagonal ribs.

Groin ribs not only solved the difficulty of the double curving groin lines seen at Vézelay, but created a consistent pattern with transverse arch ribs. The ribs could be built first over the timber formwork with carefully cut stones in a simple curved line, providing a permanent centering for the subsequent construction of the curved web sections between the ribs. The joints between the web sections were effectively concealed by the ribs, alleviating the mason of the problem of creating a clean groin line. The development of the rib was thus driven primarily by aesthetic rather than structural considerations. Indeed, examples exist of Gothic churches bombed in the wars, with webs remaining after the ribs had collapsed. The reinforcement of the rib allowed thinner and lighter webs than with a simple groin vault, however. The diagonal groin rib is thus fundamental to the development of Gothic architecture, and led to a new formal structure of diagonal geometric division and fragmentation, in opposition to the frontal, additive, and totalizing qualities of the Romanesque.[22]

EARLY GOTHIC IN FRANCE

Unifying the pointed arch and stone groin ribs is a key development during the eleventh and twelfth centuries that led to the emergence of the Gothic style.[23] A very early version of this synthesis can be seen at the Norman Durham Cathedral (1093–1133) in the north of England, but there is no evidence that it influenced the slightly later churches in the Île-de-France that are generally acknowledged as the beginning of Gothic. As opposed to the characteristic thick wall of Norman architecture, in the Île-de-France a tradition of thin-walled buildings grew, which were then wedded to pointed rib vaults. One of the earliest and most influential examples involved Abbot Suger's addition of a new choir (1140–44) to his eighth-century abbey church, the BASILICA OF SAINT-DENIS, just north of Paris. The Basilica of Saint-Denis was an important royal burial site, and as such enjoyed significant patronage from Louis VI. Suger was abbot from 1122 and a close advisor to both the king and his son, Louis VII, who succeeded in 1137. The new choir in the Basilica of Saint-Denis included an ambulatory and radiating chapels, which was to provide a strong model for subsequent Gothic churches.

Abbot Suger is unique among medieval art patrons in having left writings that point to his intentions. His famous fascination with a metaphysics of light, and the

BASILICA OF SAINT-DENIS (see p. 30)

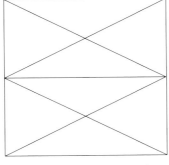

correlation of the light entering the church with the spiritual light of God, may have influenced the new skeletal wall structure with much thinner vertical members introduced in the Basilica of Saint-Denis choir, which encouraged an unusually extensive band of glazing.[24] However, the exact form of the choir built for Suger by the first Basilica of Saint-Denis master is unknown, as the upper sections of the choir were extended, the triforium glazed, and the vaulting replaced around 1231.[25]

The slightly later choir (after 1165) added to the Romanesque Basilica of St. Mary Magdalene, in Vézelay, was likely influenced by the Basilica of Saint-Denis and probably indicates the original form of Suger's choir of 1140–44.[26] Here relatively thin piers with attached shafts allow a clerestory with extensive glazing, which rises above the blind galleries of the triforium. The rectangular bays are capped by pointed rib vaults, which are probably similar to the original form of the Saint-Denis choir. The innovations at the Basilica of Saint-Denis were to have a profound influence not only on the new choir in Vézelay, but on the succeeding generation of French cathedrals, almost all of which adopted pointed rib vaults.

The Laon Cathedral (1160–1230), to the north of Paris, is one of the finest examples of early Gothic architecture in France. Although the overall design is reminiscent of the Church of Saint Étienne at Caen, with a lantern tower over the crossing (ca. 1170–75), the additional level of a blind band triforium is introduced between the main galleries and the clerestory. The ribbed vaults, sexpartite in the nave as in the Church of Saint Étienne, are continued in the aisle vaults (which are simple groin vaults in the Church of Saint Étienne). The compound piers are also a more complexly articulated type, comprised of bundles of applied shafts, each of which continues up as a rib or window arch.[27]

Much smaller windows penetrate the clerestory of the eleventh-century Romanesque Church of Saint Rémi (1005–49) in Reims, which was rebuilt with ribbed vaults in the second half of the twelfth century, roughly at the same time as Laon Cathedral.[28] Unlike the sexpartite vaults in Laon Cathedral, the vaults in the Church of Saint Rémi are quadripartite, with each rectangular bay divided by two crossing diagonal ribs into four parts. The quadripartite vault had some advantage over the sexpartite type, as its reduced angle exerted significantly less lateral force at the end of each bay, and thus required less substantial propping at the unfinished end during construction. These two differing types of simple rib vaults represent roughly concurrent alternative solutions to the same problem. However, with only a few exceptions, the quadripartite vault was to become the standard French form during the rise of Gothic architecture over the next two centuries.

Basilica of St. Mary Magdalene (see p. 31)
Laon Cathedral (see p. 29)
Church of Saint Rémi (see p. 32)
Quadripartite vault diagram

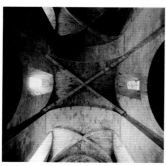

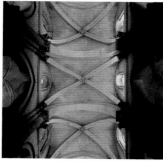

CANTERBURY CATHEDRAL (*see p. 35*)

WELLS CATHEDRAL (*see p. 33*)

SANTA MARÍA DE SANTES CREUS (*see p. 36*)

SANTA MARIA D'ALCOBAÇA (*see p. 39*)

OLD CATHEDRAL (*see p. 37*)

INTRODUCTION OF GOTHIC ARCHITECTURE TO NEIGHBORING COUNTRIES

Elements of the Gothic began to appear as relatively isolated episodes in neighboring countries during the second half of the twelfth century. In England, Archbishop Lanfranc, a former prior of the Church of Saint Étienne in Caen, had begun CANTERBURY CATHEDRAL (1066–1498) in the Norman Romanesque style.[29] When a fire in 1174 destroyed the choir of the largely completed building, the French master William of Sens was called to Canterbury to rebuild. Drawing on the latest French ideas, William commenced building a greatly enlarged choir in the new style, but he was seriously injured in a fall from the scaffolding in 1178. Although he tried to direct the works from his sickbed, this proved too difficult and he returned to his home in France. This first William was replaced by his assistant, William the Englishman, described by the cathedral's chronicler Gervase as "small in body but in workmanship of many kinds acute and honest."[30] The second William extended the building still further eastward by adding the Trinity Chapel and Corona (1175–84) (housing the shrine of the martyr Thomas Becket), which is like a circular head on the eastern termination of the cruciform plan.[31]

Other early Gothic developments in England from the end of the twelfth century include the WELLS CATHEDRAL (1180–1490) nave, which was begun in 1190 but vaulted from 1200 to 1230 by the English mason Adam Lock. Lock was probably the second master of Wells, and worked there until his death around 1229.[32] Canterbury Cathedral, however, was to be the last time a French master designed a major English cathedral, which from the thirteenth century developed particular regional characteristics.

The Cistercians helped bring the Gothic style to the Iberian Peninsula. SANTA MARÍA DE SANTES CREUS (ca. 1174–1314), a monastery church in Catalonia, is indicative of their spare and even austere version of Gothic, with Romanesque flat walls, and only the cross-ribbed vaults to betray the new style's influence.[33] Perhaps the grandest Cistercian monastery church is SANTA MARIA D'ALCOBAÇA (1178–1252) in Portugal, with cross-ribbed vaults in both the nave and the aisles.[34] Santa Maria d'Alcobaça is an example of the hall church type. While basilicas have a central space with a clerestory that is higher than the aisles, hall church aisles are roughly the same height as the central space, with the only natural light coming from windows on the external walls. Despite the lack of a clerestory, the interior of Santa Maria d'Alcobaça is still reasonably well lit by windows in the aisle walls. The OLD CATHEDRAL (1150–80) in Salamanca, Spain, also has ribbed vaults, but even with the basilica form the interior is only dimly lit by its very small clerestory windows, and the massive architectural members express the building's Romanesque pedigree.[35] Although roughly contemporary with the Cathedral of Notre-Dame in Paris, Laon Cathedral, and Canterbury Cathedral, the Spanish and

Portuguese churches appear far more archaic. Therefore, we must look to France and England for the next great developments in the Gothic style during the thirteenth century.

THE DEVELOPMENT AND SPREAD OF GOTHIC ARCHITECTURE (1160–1350)

The thirteenth century marks the rise of Gothic architecture as the dominant style for new churches in Europe, with a progressive development in both the structural and aesthetic means. In the high Gothic period in France the height limit for the thin wall was tested, with a commensurate increase in clerestory height and luminosity. A growing fascination with articulating the walls linearly enhanced this verticality, with the piers, shafts, window frames, and tracery opening the thin walls even further toward being a diaphanous, translucent membrane, like a dragonfly's wing.

HIGH GOTHIC

While most of the earliest Gothic cathedrals were no higher than the largest of their Romanesque antecedents, the CATHEDRAL OF NOTRE-DAME (1163–1250) in Paris, begun at about the same time as Laon Cathedral, is an exception. Perhaps in an assertion of Paris's capitol status, the vaults of Notre-Dame rise 109 feet (33 meters) in the central space, surpassing the heights of the Abbey of Cluny and Speyer Cathedral.[36] This quest for height was a driving force for the high Gothic cathedrals of the thirteenth century. The Cathedral of Notre-Dame retained the galleries and sexpartite vaults of the Church of Saint Étienne in Caen, with relatively small stained glass windows in the clerestory, which, from their great height, provide only dim light to the central space.

CHARTRES CATHEDRAL (1194–1260) was one of the most influential churches of the thirteenth century in France.[37] Although flying buttresses had been used previously, the master who rebuilt Chartres Cathedral after the fire of 1194 was the first to realize the structural potential of flyers to greatly strengthen the walls and thus allow an increased window area. Medieval builders' affinity for the use of stained glass had a natural dimming effect on the amount of light entering the church; increasing the window size mitigated this. Indeed, the largely original stained glass windows that almost fill the enlarged clerestory at Chartres Cathedral have a richly colored luminosity, and the large oculi at the top of the design heighten this effect. The Chartres Cathedral master built quadripartite vaults over the nave, which would become the norm in France for the next century. Although quadripartite vaults exerted less lateral force at the end of each bay, the Chartres Cathedral master took no chances and cautiously provided far greater mass in the supporting walls and buttresses than was required. The medieval architect had no knowledge of the science of engineering statics, and had to rely on rough empirical knowledge gained through experience.[38]

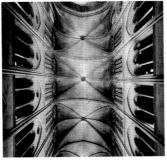

CATHEDRAL OF NOTRE-DAME (*see p. 40*)
CHARTRES CATHEDRAL (*see p. 41*)

BOURGES CATHEDRAL (*see p. 42*)
SOISSONS CATHEDRAL (*see p. 46*)
REIMS CATHEDRAL (*see p. 43*)
AMIENS CATHEDRAL (*see p. 50*)

BOURGES CATHEDRAL (1195–1255) was begun at about the same time as Chartres Cathedral, with the nave constructed between 1225 and 1255.[39] Both the sexpartite vaults and the double aisles on each side of the main space are modeled on the Cathedral of Notre-Dame, in Paris, but with greater window area and a better lit interior, and no transept. The inner aisles at Bourges Cathedral are intermediate in height between the nave and outer aisles, and have their own clerestory to provide more light. The architect also devised a much lighter supporting structure in comparison to those of the Cathedral of Notre-Dame or Chartres Cathedral, using thinner, more steeply sloped flying buttresses that transmit the outward thrusts of the high vault more efficiently to the ground.[40] It was the Chartres Cathedral model, however, that was to be far more influential, with its single aisle plan, quadripartite vaults, and high windows spawning a succession of derivations at Soissons, Reims, and Amiens.

If Bourges Cathedral can be understood as a correction of the Cathedral of Notre-Dame, then SOISSONS CATHEDRAL (1197–1479), REIMS CATHEDRAL (1211–1427), and AMIENS CATHEDRAL (1220–70) have a similar relation to Chartres Cathedral. Soissons Cathedral was begun soon after Chartres Cathedral. Though its internal height is lower than that of Chartres Cathedral—99 feet (30 meters) versus 122 feet (37 meters)—its very similar design suggests that the architect had worked on Chartres Cathedral.[41] At Soissons, however, the piers and vault supports are far lighter than at Chartres, pointing toward the even more diaphanous structures created at Reims and Amiens.

Reims Cathedral was commenced as Chartres Cathedral was nearing completion. Uncertainty surrounds the designer of Reims, and this is indicative of the scant information that remains of architects from the early Gothic period. Inscriptions on a labyrinth installed in the nave floor of Reims Cathedal are the basis of the belief that at least four architects—Jean d'Orbais, Jean (de) Loup, Gaucher de Reims, and Bernard de Soissons—were involved with the design and construction of the building between 1211 and 1310. This labyrinth, however, was destroyed in 1779 and only secondary evidence, such as drawings, remain. Besides these four, other evidence suggests that possibly a Robert de Coucy, and an even more enigmatic Adam (of Reims) were involved with the design. Whomever were ultimately responsible (and virtually nothing is known of any of them), they refined the Chartres Cathedral model by reworking the clerestory design with thinner bar tracery dividing the oculus and double windows of each bay, thus increasing the glass area and creating a more unified effect.[42]

Amiens Cathedral is sometimes seen as the apogee of the French high Gothic innovations started at Chartres Cathedral. On the basis of an inscription in the labyrinth installed in the nave in 1288 by Regnault de Cormont, the successive architects are thought to be Robert de Luzarches, Thomas de Cormont, and Regnault de Cormont.

Robert de Luzarches is believed to be responsible for the initial design, which determined the scale and aesthetic of the building.[43] In contrast to most churches, which were built from east to west, construction at Amiens Cathedral commenced with the nave, moving eastward to the crossing and choir (1269). At 141 feet (43 meters), the great height of the vaults in Amiens Cathedral was unprecedented. The clerestory windows are a further elaboration of the thin bar tracery of the Reims Cathedral pattern in that a scaled-down version of the overall window design is inserted into each of its two paired components. The resultant division of the window into seven components by the tracery signaled the increasing focus on linear detail in the French buildings.[44]

THE RAYONNANT STYLE

The choirs in BEAUVAIS CATHEDRAL (1225–1337) and COLOGNE CATHEDRAL (1248–1880) exceed even Amiens Cathedral's, both in the height of the vaults and the window design. Beauvais and Cologne herald the new Rayonnant style, dominant in France from the middle of the thirteenth century to the middle of the fourteenth century, with its emphasis on stained glass, and particularly the radiating (*rayonnant* is French for radiating) designs of rose windows. Both Beauvais Cathedral and Cologne Cathedral have a glazed triforium, further extending the verticality of the glazing and opening up and unifying the interior elevations. Glazed triforiums had been used at several lower French churches, including in the renovations to the Basilica of Saint-Denis (ca. 1216), and in Troyes Cathedral (1208–40), whose glazed triforium was added in the late 1230s. Beauvais Cathedral's vertiginous internal height, 158 feet (48 meters), is sometimes blamed for its collapse in 1284 and subsequent rebuilding with sexpartite vaults between 1284 and 1337.[45] Rather than excessive dead weight overloading the supports, however, it is more likely that the intermittent high wind loads and related tensile failures—to which extremely tall masonry structures are subject—were major contributing factors to the disaster.[46] This was not, however, the only disaster for Beauvais Cathedral. A transept and massive crossing tower was completed in the sixteenth century, which collapsed in 1573. The cathedral remains incomplete to this day.[47]

In Cologne Cathedral, the towering choir—152 feet (46 meters)—was the only section of the cathedral completed in the Middle Ages. Despite being outside of France, Cologne Cathedral is a superlative example of the Rayonnant style. The glazed triforium leads to an expansive clerestory with elaborate window tracery designs probably derived from both Amiens Cathedral and SAINTE-CHAPPELLE (1242–48) in Paris.[48] The palace chapel of Sainte-Chappelle, built for Louis IX to house relics, is perhaps the quintessential example of the Rayonnant style. The stained glass and elaborate window tracery of the almost floor-to-ceiling windows of the upper chapel create the most dramatic effect of a luminous glass cage.[49] This interest in Rayonnant fine tracery can also

BEAUVAIS CATHEDRAL (*see p. 54*)
COLOGNE CATHEDRAL (*see p. 55*)
SAINTE-CHAPPELLE (*see p. 57*)
BASILICA OF SAINT-URBAIN (*see p. 59*)

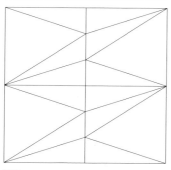

SALISBURY CATHEDRAL (*see p. 61*)

LINCOLN CATHEDRAL "CRAZY VAULTS" (*see p. 65*)

DIAGRAM OF ST. HUGH'S CHOIR VAULT

LINCOLN CATHEDRAL NAVE (*see p. 66*)

LINCOLN CATHEDRAL ANGEL CHOIR (*see p. 68*)

be seen in the elaborate detailing of all aspects of the highly skeletonized structure of the collegiate BASILICA OF SAINT-URBAIN (1262–86) in Troyes.[50]

THE EARLY ENGLISH STYLE AND ITS INFLUENCE: TIERCERON AND PALM VAULTS

While in France the quadripartite vault was conservatively maintained throughout the high Gothic period, in England the architectural exploration of linear pattern found its expression in the invention of ever more complex rib designs for the vaults, which were to have a profound influence on late Gothic architecture. This is not yet evident, however, in the conservative quadripartite vaults at SALISBURY CATHEDRAL (1220–58).[51] The Lady Chapel at Salisbury was built first, followed by the eastern arm and transepts, and finally the nave and great transepts, all probably designed and completed by Nicholas of Ely, thought to be master of works from 1220 to 1258.[52] Salisbury was the only cathedral built on a new site in England during the Gothic period, freeing it from the constraints of adding on to existing foundations, which hampered so many other projects.[53] The treatment of the interior wall elevations at Salisbury Cathedral, WORCESTER CATHEDRAL (1084–1396) (see pages 62–63), LINCOLN CATHEDRAL (1185–1311), and other thirteenth-century English cathedrals show their clear debt to the pronounced galleries of the late Anglo-Norman Romanesque. The clerestories are much lower in these buildings than their contemporary French counterparts, and the glazing far less prominent, suggesting that horizontality rather than verticality was a particularity of English architectural expression. Even the characteristic English ridge rib reinforces the flow of horizontal movement. Ridge ribs, which run along either the longitudinal or transverse crowns of the vault, had first appeared in France in the middle of the twelfth century. It was in England, however, that the ridge rib came to be exploited most fully for its decorative effect.

Instead of focusing on an ever-increasing height in their churches, thirteenth-century English architects and builders experimented with various vault designs, leading to the invention of a new kind of vault: the tierceron. These innovations began with the extraordinary "crazy vaults" of St. Hugh's Choir (1192–1200) in Lincoln Cathedral, probably designed by mason Geoffrey de Noyer.[54] The central ridge of the choir vault is strongly defined by a ridge rib, and instead of the standard four diagonal ribs, six ribs meet the ridge rib in an eccentric fashion, dividing each bay into six parts in an alternating pattern that lends a fascinating asymmetry to the design and breaks down the division of bays. The term *tierceron vault* is derived from the additional, decorative third rib.

In Lincoln Cathedral's slightly later nave (1225–53), built by Alexander the Mason III, the asymmetry is left behind, but multiple splayed ribs spring from a single haunch to join the lateral ridge rib and short transverse ridge ribs, to create some of the first

tierceron star vaults.[55] Master Alexander (who was also active at Worcester Cathedral, and may have been the same person as Alexander the Mason II) was probably in charge of the cathedral works from about 1235 to 1256, when the nave and chapter house were built, along with the lower parts of the square crossing tower, which were reconstructed after its collapse in 1237. An even more elaborate arrangement was carried out by Richard de Stow to create an eight-pointed star in the vault of the Lincoln crossing tower (1306–11) (see page 67). Stow was subordinate to Master Simon of Thirsk until about 1291, who had executed similar tierceron star designs in the vaults of the Angel Choir (1275–90) in Lincoln Cathedral.[56]

In EXETER CATHEDRAL's nave vault (1353–69), eleven ribs rise from a single springing point, with half meeting bosses on the transverse ridge rib, and half meeting bosses on the full lateral ridge ribs that join opposite window arches. The Exeter vault was probably designed by master mason Richard Farleigh, also active on the great tower and spire at Salisbury, although Thomas Witney, the master who built the lower parts of the nave between 1328 and 1342, may also have been involved.[57] These ribs no longer define only the vaulting compartment boundaries, but decorate the entire surface of the vault.

The vault of the LINCOLN CATHEDRAL CHAPTER HOUSE (1220–35) by Master Alexander, is another more centralized version of these star vaults.[58] Drawing on a tradition of centralized chapter houses in England, Alexander built twenty ribs that radiate from the central supporting column to cross ridge ribs that form a ten-sided polygon and then regroup as star vaults around the perimeter of the ten-sided chapter house—the effect is that of a ten-pointed star. In the later WELLS CATHEDRAL CHAPTER HOUSE (1298–1305), the arrangement is similar but with thirty-two radiating ribs crossing an octagonal ridge rib and then regrouping at the eight external piers of the octagonal building to form an eight-pointed star.[59]

These new forms of vaults were to exert a strong influence both inside and outside of England over the course of the next two centuries. Even in France, where the traditional quadripartite vault remained the norm, these new more complex vaults can be found. When the choir (1275–92) of the Dominican CHURCH OF THE JACOBINS (1229–1350) in Toulouse was vaulted with the existing supports of five central columns, the column at the apse end was used to support a complicated "palm" vault, which clearly has its origins in the centralized designs of vaulted English chapter houses. The nave (1323–35) was vaulted in a more conventional but complimentary fashion.[60]

In the nearby town of Albi, the CATHEDRAL OF SAINTE-CÉCILE (1282–1480) was built to a plan equally uncommon in French churches. Fortresslike on the outside, its very wide nave on the inside is a single large space. Rather than low aisles with a clerestory, shallow open lateral chapels have windows that light the interior.[61] Unusual

EXETER CATHEDRAL (*see p. 69*)
LINCOLN CATHEDRAL CHAPTER HOUSE (*see p. 70*)
WELLS CATHEDRAL CHAPTER HOUSE (*see p. 71*)
CHURCH OF THE JACOBINS (*see p. 73*)
CATHEDRAL OF SAINTE-CÉCILE (*see p. 75*)

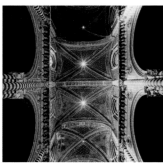

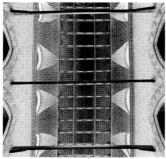

for France, all the interior surfaces are heavily decorated including the very wide quadripartite vaults.

The Spread of the Gothic Style from France to Neighboring Countries (1220–1350)

The thirteenth and fourteenth centuries saw the gradual spread of the Gothic style to France's neighbors. Italy was slow to embrace the new style, perhaps because of the strong Romanesque tradition and the traditional popularity of fresco painting to decorate the flat wall surfaces. The BASILICA OF SAN FRANCESCO D'ASSISI (1228–53), in Assisi, was built on two levels to house the saint's shrine.[62] The Gothic influence is reflected in the upper church's pointed transverse ribs and square quadripartite vaults. However, the most remarkable aspect of the building is in the Romanesque tradition: the stunning frescoes by Giotto and others that cover all the interior surfaces.

The SIENA CATHEDRAL (ca. 1226–1370) nave shows little Gothic influence. Though the walls were heightened and rib vaults added (ca. 1340–48), the vaults have conservative semicircular arches and, despite the enormous hexagonal crossing dome, the interior of the cathedral is extremely dark, owing to the clerestory's small windows.[63] ORVIETO CATHEDRAL (1280–1368) is of an even more conservative transitional Romanesque-Gothic style. The alternating bands of light and dark stone coursing, typical of many of the churches of Emilia-Romagna and Tuscany, emphasize the horizontality of the nave. The wall treatment is flat in the Romanesque manner, with only small windows penetrating the clerestory, and topped by an open timber truss roof.

Timber ceilings in churches continued to be common in Italy long after masonry vaulting was almost mandatory in other parts of Europe. In the CHURCH OF SANTO STEFANO (1325–74), in Venice, for example, the flat unarticulated walls were capped by an elaborate timber ceiling constructed *a carena di nave*, like a ship's hull.[64] Gothic church architecture did make some impact in Venice, however, with the building of the large Dominican BASILICA DEI SANTI GIOVANNI E PAULO (1333–1430).[65] Here quadripartite rib vaults were built over the almost square bays, which are separated from each other and the high aisles by pointed arches. The plain wall treatment is, however, still essentially unarticulated and the crossing dome and small clerestory windows betray the building's Romanesque parentage. In general, the Gothic style had less of an impact on church architecture in Italy than in other parts of Europe, with the Renaissance already beginning to be felt by the fifteenth century, perhaps because its classical principles were more closely linked to Roman and Romanesque precedents.

Spain also saw the growth of Gothic architecture during the fourteenth century. The impressive parish church of SANTA MARIA DEL MAR (1329–83), in Barcelona—designed and built by Berenguer de Montagut, Ramon Despuig, and Guillem

BASILICA OF SAN FRANCESCO D'ASSISI (*see p. 76*)

SIENA CATHEDRAL (*see p. 77*)

ORVIETO CATHEDRAL (*see p. 78*)

CHURCH OF SANTO STEFANO (*see p. 79*)

BASILICA DEI SANTI GIOVANNI E PAULO (*see p. 81*)

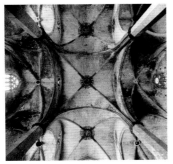

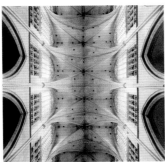

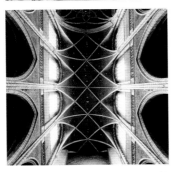

Santa Maria del Mar (*see p. 82*)
St. Rombaut's Cathedral (*see p. 84*)
Saint Bavo's Cathedral (*see p. 85*)
Cathedral of Our Lady (*see p. 87*)

Metge—has a wide nave that is divided into four great square rib vaulted bays, with simple octagonal columns separating the wide arcades.[66] The aisles are almost as high as the central space, so the very low clerestory allows only the small windows typical of Mediterranean churches. Most remarkable, however, are the larger high windows of the aisles, which are easily visible through the open arcades. This has the most dramatic effect in the ambulatory, because of its unusual height and the close spacing of windows. This is unusual for Spanish Gothic churches, which are typically very dimly lit because of their small clerestory windows.

Churches built in the fourteenth-century Netherlands, or Low Countries, particularly in Brabant, show their debt to French Rayonnant models. In Mechelen in present-day Belgium, the former collegiate church of St. Rombaut's Cathedral (1342), was built, perhaps by Jean d'Oisy, in the so-called Brabant Gothic style, typified by detailed latticework patterns in the triforium and the enlarged clerestory of Rayonnant elevations; the vault is a standard French quadripartite type.[67]

Saint Bavo's Cathedral (ca. 1200–1400)—originally called St. John—in Ghent, Belgium, has Rayonnant elevations, albeit with a reduced triforium, but the vault, which probably derives from a remodeling in the fifteenth century, also suggests an English influence.[68] The diagonal ribs here cross two bays in the manner of a sexpartite vault rather than crossing to the immediately adjacent support. This so-called net vault divides each bay into one diamond-shaped and six triangular-shaped cells.

The impressive Cathedral of Our Lady (1352–1531) in Antwerp is in the Brabant Gothic style.[69] The elevations, with the detailed tracery of the enlarged triforium and clerestory, are characteristically Rayonnant, but the exceptionally long bays are almost square in shape. While the bays have standard quadripartite vaults, the crossing has an elaborate domed octagonal lantern tower with a circular ceiling painting of later origin.

The Mature English Styles (1300–1485): Lierne Vaults

The fourteenth and fifteenth centuries in England saw further experimentation with new kinds of ribbed vaults within the mature English styles known as the Decorated (ca. 1300–50) and the Perpendicular (ca. 1330–1485). The influence of French Rayonnant was seen in increasingly elaborate window tracery, which in the Decorated style characteristically used S-curved or so-called ogee arches, whose convex-curved sides rise to concave curves terminating in a sharp point. This was succeeded by the Perpendicular style, when the tracery became simpler again and vertical lines were emphasized. With these mature English styles, the decorative patterning of the tracery also began to extend to the surface of the vaults. The tierceron star vaults first seen at Lincoln Cathedral were elaborated elsewhere with the addition of short liernes—decorative connecting ribs

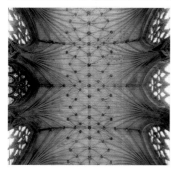

running between the splayed ribs, which are not attached to either a supporting point or a ridge rib. In WELLS CATHEDRAL'S LADY CHAPEL (1320–40)—probably built by master mason Thomas Witney (also active at Winchester and Exeter Cathedrals)—an eight-pointed star vault covers the unusual, eccentrically elongated octagonal plan, with the vault's center emphasized by two concentric stars formed by short lierne ribs.[70] These liernes serve a purely ornamental function, reinforcing the quasi-centralized structure.

Square crossing towers and centrally planned polygonal chapter houses also lent themselves to concentric liernes. The octagonal YORK MINSTER CHAPTER HOUSE (ca. 1286–96) was built with a timber vault, whose lighter weight dispensed with the need for the central support column used at Lincoln Cathedral Chapter House and Wells Cathedral Chapter House.[71] This eight-pointed vault imitates the structure of English stone vaults, with ridge ribs, tierceron ribs, and a concentric circle of liernes defining the center. The large surrounding windows with elaborate geometric tracery show the influence of the Rayonnant style, and beautifully illuminate the open interior created by the elimination of the central column. The PETERBOROUGH CATHEDRAL lantern tower (1325, rebuilt 1883–86) at the crossing has an extremely complex eight-pointed star vault that is related to that of the crossing tower at Lincoln Cathedral, but with the addition of an increased number of tierceron ribs and concentric arrangements of liernes.[72]

The Romanesque square crossing tower in ELY CATHEDRAL (1083–1375), had collapsed in 1322 and was replaced by a most extraordinary octagonal crossing tower (1322–46), known as the Octagon. The plan's origin was ascribed in the abbey's records to Alan of Walsingham, the monk responsible for the building's upkeep. There is no doubt, however, that the royal master carpenter, William Hurley, designed and built the amazing eight-pointed timber vault (1326–34) over the crossing.[73] Hurley was also responsible for the choir stalls at Ely, as well as being associated with major works at St. Stephen's Chapel at Westminster Palace, and Windsor Castle.[74] Surmounted by an elaborate octagonal lantern, the enormous span of the timber structure is supported by a complex system of concealed timber trusses. Like the York Minster Chapter House, the Ely Cathedral Octagon would have been impossible to build with the weight of stone, but the decorative tierceron star vaults nonetheless create the convincing illusion—and prestige—of a stone vault. The prevalence of imitative timber vaults in England during this period points to the sophistication of medieval English carpentry, and the ready interchange of design ideas between the master carpenters and masons.

The Ely Cathedral Lady Chapel (1321–49) was built at about the same time as the Octagon, possibly by the mason John Wysbeck.[75] The interior is a "glass cage" that is reminiscent of Sainte-Chappelle in Paris, with elaborate tracery in the floor-to-ceiling

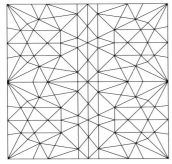

WELLS CATHEDRAL (*see p. 94*)

GLOUCESTER CATHEDRAL (*see p. 95*)

DIAGRAM OF GLOUCESTER CATHEDRAL CHOIR VAULT

YORK MINSTER CROSSING (*see p. 97*)

YORK MINSTER NAVE (*see p. 96*)

windows that fill the walls. An equally elaborate pattern of lierne ribs connects the tierceron ribs, creating a netlike web along the apex of the flattened vault.

Further elaborations of the Ely Cathedral Lady Chapel vault were executed in the WELLS CATHEDRAL choir (ca. 1329–45) and GLOUCESTER CATHEDRAL choir (1337–67), where the vaulting extends the linear patterning of the fine elevation tracery. The Wells Cathedral choir vault was probably built by the master mason William Joy, who took charge of Wells in 1329. Joy is also associated with work at Exeter, where he succeeded Thomas Witney as master, and possibly also at Bristol Cathedral.[76] The vault is essentially tunnel shaped, with transverse ribs that barely maintain the bay divisions.[77] The ridge rib, along with the tiercerons and parts of the diagonals, was eliminated. A complex arrangement of liernes creates a pattern of hexagons and squares with an even greater impression of a net than in the Ely Cathedral Lady Chapel.

The system of diagonals, tiercerons, liernes, and three parallel ridge ribs in the choir of Gloucester Cathedral is even more complicated, creating an almost unfathomably complex web vault. The strong verticals of the piers, triforium, and window tracery rise up to dissipate into a dense pattern of energetic linearity that activates the entire surface of the tunnel vault. The Gloucester Cathedral choir was possibly vaulted to the design of the king's chief mason, William Ramsey III.[78] The Ramseys were a large family of master masons, based in both London and Norwich, and William Ramsey III, who was also associated with major works at Old St. Paul's Cathedral in London, Lichfield Cathedral, and St. Stephen's Chapel at Westminster, is important as one of the key formulators of the Perpendicular style, which became influential from the middle of the fourteenth century.[79] The attention to elaborate detail characteristic of the Decorated style began to be replaced by the more pared-down aesthetic of the Perpendicular, which had a dominant influence on English church architecture until the end of the fifteenth century.

The French origins of these mature English elevations can be seen in the YORK MINSTER nave (1292–1345), whose triforium and clerestory were a fairly pure enactment of the Rayonnant style.[80] The bays are well defined, with the tracery of the triforium and the clerestory windows forming integrated units. However, instead of using the standard quadripartite vaults as originally intended, which would have maintained the strong bay divisions, Philip Lincoln, the master carpenter from 1346, vaulted the nave (1354–70) in a timber copy of an English stone lierne vault, perhaps drawing on the earlier timber vault of the York Minster Chapter House.[81] The network of diagonal and ridge ribs creates a smooth dissipation of the vertical forces across the surface of the shallow vault to soften the bay divisions. Master William Colchester (also associated with works at Westminster Abbey) built the square lantern tower (1407–23) that rises over the massive piers of the crossing, with vaulting (1470–74) by William Hyndeley,

CANTERBURY CATHEDRAL (*see p. 98*)
WINCHESTER CATHEDRAL (*see p. 100*)

originally from Norwich, who was warden of the York Minster masons' lodge from 1473 until his death in 1505.[82]

Both CANTERBURY CATHEDRAL nave (1379–1405) and WINCHESTER CATHEDRAL nave (1394–1450) were a remodeling of earlier Romanesque structures, and are indicative of the shift to the Perpendicular style. The design of the Canterbury Cathedral nave was probably by the highly successful London-based Henry Yeveley, one of the greatest English mason-architects of the fourteenth century, who was also responsible for the nave at Westminster Abbey, among many other works.[83] The rib design at Canterbury Cathedral is much sparser than that of the Gloucester Cathedral choir, using octagonal arrangements of liernes to reinforce the lateral ridge as well as the transverse bays, and was erected in 1400, the year of Yeveley's death.

At Winchester Cathedral the vaults over the nave were built by William Wynford, and relate closely to Yeveley's design at Canterbury.[84] Wynford was master mason at both Winchester Cathedral and Wells Cathedral (where he had succeeded William Joy) from 1360 to 1403. The crossing vault (1475–90) at Winchester was built in a similar style somewhat later.[85] The liernes create diamond shapes along the apex, following approximate arcs around the conoids formed by the splayed tierceron ribs, anticipating the blind tracery designs of the later fan vaults characteristic of the sixteenth century in England.[86]

THE FLAMBOYANT STYLE (1380–1500)

In France, the Rayonnant style gave way in the late Gothic period to the Flamboyant style, characterized by its "flamelike" tracery, related to similar curving tracery designs that had appeared somewhat earlier in the English Decorated style. Although there were few major new projects, windows were frequently replaced in the Flamboyant style, including rose windows at Amiens Cathedral (ca. 1500), Beauvais Cathedral, and Sainte-Chappelle in Paris. Flamboyant tracery designs also found their way abroad, and were influential in Spain from the mid-fifteenth century, such as the tracery of the Constable's Chapel (1482–94) at Burgos Cathedral.

LATE GOTHIC ARCHITECTURE IN CENTRAL EUROPE (1300–1550): NET VAULTS, DOUBLE-CURVED RIBS, AND DIAMOND VAULTS

The Gothic style flourished in Central Europe during the late Gothic period, with many of the most exciting innovations in vault design found in churches built in the regions of present-day Germany and the Czech Republic. Especially in Central Europe, the large number of churches built in the late Middle Ages was primarily due to the enormous growth of towns. Affluence and civic pride fueled a competitive surge in the construction of parish churches, sometimes of a scale rivaling the cathedrals. For example, from

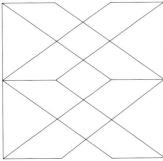

St. Mary's Church (*see p. 103*)

Bad Doberan Minster (*see p. 104*)

St. Vitus Cathedral (*see p. 106*)

Diagram of nave vault, St. Vitus Cathedral

Church of St. Sebaldus (*see p. 109*)

the thirteenth to the fifteenth century, the town of Lübeck, Germany, was the most powerful economic force in the geographically huge Baltic region. Lübeck's preeminence was assured after it had assumed leadership of the Hanseatic League of towns, which had a virtual monopoly on Northern European trade. Strong trading links with Flanders, and indeed the Flemish origin of many of Lübeck's citizens, may explain the spread to the Baltic of a French-related version of Gothic churches, which had ambulatories with radiating chapels.[87]

The large parish St. Mary's Church (1277–1351), in Lübeck, is built in the local brick tradition and has an impressive internal height—128 feet (39 meters)—that exceeds Chartres Cathedral and approaches that of Amiens, Cologne, and Beauvais cathedrals.[88] Although lacking the triforium of the French and Flemish models, the tall clerestory provides ample light to the spacious interior. In contrast to the French and Flemish churches, the interior of the brick building is covered with decorative paintwork, a tradition that was continued in the series of copies of St. Mary's Church that were built along the Baltic Sea during the succeeding century. The former Cistercian monastery church of Bad Doberan Minster (1294–1368) near Rostock, Germany, has decorative paintwork that harmonizes with the brick interior.[89] There is even a false triforium executed in paintwork between the arcades and the clerestory.

After the extraordinary example of the Rayonnant style at Cologne Cathedral, St. Vitus Cathedral (1344–1929), in Prague, was the most significant Gothic basilica built to the French plan in Central Europe. With the wealth of silver mining during the fourteenth century, the Bohemian kings transformed Prague into an eastern Paris and built the first university north of the Alps. Emperor Charles IV founded St. Vitus Cathedral after negotiating with the pope for the establishment of Prague as an archdiocese. Matthias of Arras was the building's first architect and designed it in a Rayonnant manner, but he died in 1352. The talented twenty-three-year-old Peter Parler of Gmünd (probably the son of master mason Heinrich Parler, active at Schwäbisch Gmünd) took over in 1356. Construction of St. Vitus Cathedral continued until 1420, when it stopped due to the Hussite revolution, with the nave incomplete until the early twentieth century.[90] Parler designed the high tunnel vaults with net patterns that may derive from slightly earlier precedents in England, such as the previously discussed choir vault in Wells Cathedral. Like in Wells Cathedral, the diagonal ribs cross two bays, and sections are left out to create net-like polygons—diamonds in St. Vitus Cathedral, as compared to the squares and hexagons in the Wells Cathedral choir.

The net vaults of St. Vitus Cathedral were highly influential on later Gothic architecture in Central Europe, especially in the form of the hall church, which was widespread in many parts of present-day Germany. The Church of St. Sebaldus (1359–79) in Nuremberg is an early example of a German hall church.[91] The

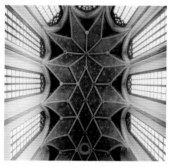

vaulting is of the conservative quadripartite type, with two closely spaced piers at the apse end. A later alternative to this arrangement can be seen at both the CHURCH OF THE HOLY SPIRIT (1407–61) in Landshut, and the CHURCH OF ST. JOHN (1467–1502) in Dingolfing, where the apse end has a single pier, maintaining a more constant pier spacing.[92] As with many fifteenth-century German hall churches, the net vaults with their pattern of closely spaced ribs show a growing sophistication in the experimentation with English-derived forms.

In the CHURCH OF ST. MARTIN (1385–1480), in Landshut, the choir was built first by Hanns Krummenauer, with a complex vault. He was succeeded in the nave by Hanns Purhauser, with a vault that is an almost identical copy of Peter Parler's vaults in St. Vitus Cathedral. Purhauser was one of the great German architects of the period, who also designed the main parish church in Salzburg.[93] This tendency toward increasing vault complexity in Central Europe over the course of the fifteenth and sixteenth centuries is even more apparent in the HOLY CROSS CATHEDRAL (1315–1521) in Schwäbisch Gmünd. The church was begun as early as 1315, probably by Peter Parler's father, Heinrich, who along with his son, may also have designed the choir. The choir vault was rebuilt later (1497–1521) after a collapse of the towers, possibly by another great German architect of the period, Burkhard Engelberg.[94] The English lineage of these decorative vaults is apparent in the nave, where the design is close to that of the Lady Chapel in Ely Cathedral. The choir is more complex still, with a dense net vault reminiscent of the Gloucester Cathedral choir.

In Vienna, the huge ST. STEPHEN'S CATHEDRAL (1359–1467) (see page 117) is a modified hall church design, with the nave only slightly higher than the aisles, and no clerestory. Construction continued over a century and a half, with the net vault over the nave completed to a design by Hans Puchspaum.[95] Similar designs from the same time period can be seen in the CHURCH OF ST. GEORGE (1448–99) (see page 118) in Dinkelsbühl, built by Niclaus Eseler the Elder and his son Niclaus Eseler the Younger, and in the FRAUENKIRCHE (1468–94) in Munich, built by Jörg Ganghofer (also known as Jorg von Halsbach).[96] Ganghofer was the city architect in Munich, where he also worked on the old town hall. Little is known of him, except that he was born near Moosberg, Germany and died in 1488, at which time the Frauenkirche, his most important building, was complete (except for the tower). The Frauenkirche is one of the most beautiful examples of the German hall church type, achieving a highly refined sense of balance and harmony with its very high interior, lines of octagonal piers, and stellar pattern vault.

In the fifteenth century, the decorative net vaults of German hall churches reach perhaps their highest expression in two buildings, one in the small town of Pirna toward the Czech border east of Dresden, and the other slightly further south in Annaberg-Buchholz. ST. MARY'S CHURCH (1502–46) in Pirna has octagonal piers similar to the

CHURCH OF THE HOLY SPIRIT (see p. 110)
CHURCH OF ST. JOHN (see p. 111)
CHURCH OF ST. MARTIN (see p. 113)
HOLY CROSS CATHEDRAL (see p. 115)
FRAUENKIRCHE (see p. 119)

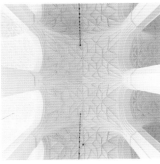

St. Mary's Church Pirna (see p. 120)

St. Anne's Church (see p. 121)

St. Mary's Church Stargard Szczeciński (see p. 125)

St. Mary's Church Gdańsk (see p. 127)

St. Bridget's Church (see p. 129)

Munich Frauenkirche.[97] The aisles display a pattern of star vaults, which coalesces in the tunnel vault of the nave to a densely meshlike rectilinear rib pattern, similar to that of the choir at Schwäbisch Gmünd. The vault surfaces between the ribs are lavishly decorated with painted floral motifs.

The floral design is carried further still in St. Anne's Church (1499–1525) in Annaberg-Buchholz, whose vault (1519–22), though related to star vaults, is one of the earliest examples of a double-curved rib design.[98] Here, besides following the curved profile of the vault, the ribs also curve horizontally to create centralized flower patterns with six petal-like cells. This botanical analogy is further reinforced by the double-curved ribs appearing to grow out of the octagonal piers like the branches of a plant.

In Bohemia, a very similar petal-like pattern was used for the nave vault of the Cathedral of St. Barbara (1388–1548) (see page 122) at Kutná Hora in the present-day Czech Republic. The wealth from the local silver mines funded a basilica begun by Peter Parler with a clerestory of the French type and star-pattern vaults over the choir. The south German master Benedikt Ried added the upper parts of the nave (1540–48), with the windows so strongly recessed as to provide hidden lighting to the extraordinary vault, which has a rib design extremely close to the slightly earlier one in Annaberg.[99] Ried is credited with the earliest example of this kind of double-curved rib vault, in the Vladislav Hall of Prague Castle (1493–1514), which provided the model for the later ones at Annaberg and Kutná Hora.

The blending of star and flower patterns in the vaults can also be seen along the Baltic Sea. At Stargard Szczeciński in present-day Poland, St. Mary's Church (1292–1500) is a unique brick basilica with a triforium designed by Hinrich Brunsberg, with vaults that have a basic star pattern modified by curving lierne ribs to create petal-like configurations.[100] Perhaps deriving from Peter Parler's earlier choir in Kutná Hora, these decorative effects are further enhanced by the painted patterns on the vaults, which extend to the extensive painted star patterns of the ambulatory vaults.

Further east, in Gdańsk, the enormous brick St. Mary's Church (1379–1502) was vaulted (1496–1502) by Heinrich Haetzl.[101] While the nave has ribbed vaults in a star pattern, in the aisles the raised ribs were eliminated and the cell divisions retained, creating a faceted form known as a cell or diamond vault. Haetzl's vaults were influential in Gdansk, where they were copied at other parish churches such as St. Catherine's and St. Bridget's (ca. 1500). These unusual ribless faceted diamond vaults seem to have first been used by Arnold von Westfalen, the highly innovative architect of Albrechtsburg Castle (1470s) in Meissen near Dresden. From there they spread through Bohemia to other parts of Central Europe.[102] In Tábor in the present-day Czech Republic, Master Stanek of Prague vaulted the choir of the Dean Church of Lord's Conversion on Mount Tábor (ca. 1480–1512) (see page 128) with similar diamond vaults.[103]

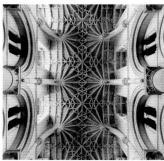

NORWICH CATHEDRAL (*see p. 131*)

CHRIST CHURCH CATHEDRAL (*see p. 132*)

BATH ABBEY (*see p. 135*)

CANTERBURY CATHEDRAL (*see p. 99*)

KING'S COLLEGE CHAPEL (*see p. 133*)

THE LATE ENGLISH STYLE (1480–1550): PENDANT VAULTS AND FAN VAULTS

Late Gothic architects in England continued to experiment with new vault forms throughout the fifteenth and sixteenth centuries. The late Perpendicular vaults (1472–99) over the choir of NORWICH CATHEDRAL, designed by Robert Everard, master from 1440 to 1485, show an arrangement of liernes that creates star patterns down the apex of the vault.[104] The transition from the rounded Norman arcades is handled in an interesting manner: the rounded arch forms and attached half shafts are echoed by the double compound columns of the clerestory, joined at the top by arches from which the ribs spring.

Another solution to the transition from a Norman lower elevation to a late Gothic vault can be seen in CHRIST CHURCH CATHEDRAL (1158–1529) in Oxford. Here the architect (probably William Orchard, active at Oxford from 1475 until he died in 1504) built the vault (1478–1503) with an even more complex star pattern of liernes than at Norwich Cathedral.[105] The ribs spring from pendants attached to ridged brackets that curve up and out from the heavy Norman arcades. These hanging pendants have no function whatsoever but are purely decorative embellishments and lead directly to the pendant fan vaults of the Tudor period.

The fine curvilinear motifs of fan vaults, whose carved ribs are equally spaced and of the same curvature, signal the end of the Perpendicular style and the beginning of the Tudor period in English architecture. By the sixteenth century the carving of standardized components was well established in the masons' workshops, and fan vaults are partially a reflection of this. In traditional Gothic vaults the ribs were separate components constructed first as a permanent centering for the webs, which were composed of individual cut blocks overlaid subsequently on the rib structure. With fan vaults the ribs are an integral blind tracery pattern carved into large, shell-like curved plates. These could be carved in the workshop as standardized modules, which were then fitted together on site to form the vault.

Among the most extraordinary examples of this type of vault are those found in BATH ABBEY (1501–39), designed by Robert and William Vertue, the sons of Adam Vertue, who was employed as a mason at Westminster Abbey. The Vertue brothers both had appointments as master masons for the king and were the preeminent designers of late Gothic fan vaults in England. They are associated with the designs of the vaults of Henry VII's Chapel in Westminster Abbey and St. George's Chapel in Windsor Castle.[106]

Fan vaults were also used by John Wastell in the Bell Harry Tower (1493–1507) built over the crossing of CANTERBURY CATHEDRAL. Wastell was one the most significant masons of the late Gothic period in England who did not hold a royal appointment and is attributed with the fan vaults in KING'S COLLEGE CHAPEL (1448–1515) at

Cambridge, added in 1508–15.[107] The interior of King's College Chapel is extraordinarily beautiful, with the delicate tracery of the enormous stained glass windows of the aisleless choir taken up perfectly by the fan vault's delicate blind tracery.

Interestingly, English fan vaults are contemporary with the Central European double-curved rib vaults in St. Anne's Church at Annaberg and the nave of the Cathedral of St. Barbara in Kutná Hora, as well as the late Gothic vaults of Portugal and Spain. Although of radically different types, all use curved motifs derived from the arcs of circles, a characteristic also echoed by the Italian Renaissance's return at the same time to classical forms based on the circle.

Late Gothic in Portugal and Spain (1380–1590) and the Beginning of the Renaissance

The Gothic style slowly took hold on the Iberian Peninsula over the course of the fourteenth century, having a final flowering in the late Gothic period. Under the Catholic monarchs, elaborately decorative court styles developed in the late fifteenth and early sixteenth centuries, known as the Isabelline style (after Queen Isabella) in Spain, and the Manueline style (after King Manuel I) in Portugal.

King João I of Portugal founded the impressive Dominican monastery and royal burial chapels of Santa Maria da Vitória (1388–1533) in Batalha.[108] The large scale of Afonso Domingues's design looks back to Santa Maria d'Alcobaça. Domingues died in 1402, when Master Huguet (possibly of English origin) took over the work, increasing the height of the nave and building the vaults. While the elevations suggest French models, the ridge ribs of the vaults over both the nave and the aisles are more English in character. This is particularly true of the complicated choir vault, which is divided into sixteen compartments by the diagonal and ridge ribs, and the superimposition of a diamond shape over the choir's two rectangular bays. Huguet also designed the two burial chapels attached to the church, before he died in 1440. The square Founder's Chapel (1426–34) was to house the tombs of King João I and his wife, while the huge circular building, intended as the resting place of King Duarte I and his family, was never completed, hence the name the Unfinished Chapels (begun 1435).[109] Probably intended to have a beautiful eight-pointed stellar vault like its sister, the Unfinished Chapels now have only the vault of the sky.

Near Lisbon, King Manuel I founded the Church of Santa Maria (1501–1572) at the Hieronymite Monastery in Belém, built to a design by Diogo Boytac, who also designed the Franciscan church at Setúbal and may have been involved with the late works at Batalha. The nave at Belém was completed around 1517 by João de Castilho, who was active at Belém until about 1530.[110] Slender piers support a vault of complex stellar design, containing both straight and curved ribs.

Santa Maria da Vitória (*see p. 138*)
Santa Maria da Vitória Founder's Chapel (*see p. 140*)
Santa Maria da Vitória Unfinished Chapels (*see p. 141*)
Church of Santa Maria (*see p. 143*)

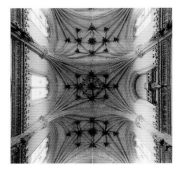

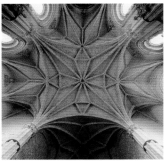

In Spain, victory at the Battle of Toro and the birth of a royal heir were commemorated by the founding of the Franciscan monastery of SAN JUAN DE LOS REYES in Toledo, with the church (1477–99) intended as the funerary chapel for Ferdinand and Isabella. Juan Guas, one of the most important Spanish architects of his generation, built the church after he had already completed the Hieronymite monastery of SANTA MARÍA DEL PARRAL (1455–75) in Segovia.[111] Typical of most Spanish Gothic churches, at San Juan de los Reyes the nave vault design of strongly defined transverse ribs and tierceron star vaults connected in the center of each bay by short ridge ribs and liernes reinforces the autonomy of each bay, rather than the unifying lateral flow down the apex of the vault that characterizes contemporary English and German designs. The stellar-vaulted octagonal crossing tower at San Juan de los Reyes continues a Spanish tradition of circular or octagonal crossing towers, often influenced by Islamic designs, which can also be seen at Burgos.

BURGOS CATHEDRAL (1221–1569) has the most remarkable octagonal crossing tower (1466–1502), first built by the German-born architect Juan de Colonia, who was active at Burgos from 1442. The open-lattice lantern tower (1569) seen now is thought to be a faithful copy of the original, which had collapsed in 1539.[112] The amazing stellar vault of the tower suggests a debt to the Islamic designs easily visible in Andalusia, which exerted a strong influence on Spanish Gothic. The Colonia family was famous for these impressive open-lattice lantern towers, despite the structural problems they exhibited. Juan's son Simón built a similar open-lattice vault over the Constable's Chapel (1482–1505) at Burgos, as well as one over the crossing of Seville Cathedral (1497–1502), which collapsed in 1511.

During the fifteenth and sixteenth centuries, wealth from the Americas helped build a series of impressive Gothic cathedrals in Seville, Salamanca, Palencia, and Segovia. The CATHEDRAL OF SANTA MARIA (ca. 1402–1515) in Seville was begun early in the fifteenth century, but the extremely active Juan Gil de Hontañón, who was also involved with Palencia, Salamanca, and Segovia cathedrals, did not complete the elaborate vaults built to replace Simón de Colonia's collapsed crossing tower until more than a century later.[113] Due to the very broad aisles and absence of a clerestory, the Cathedral of Santa Maria is even darker inside than most Spanish cathedrals.

The cathedrals at Palencia, Salamanca, and Segovia are all of a related basilica type with aisles and clerestory, and have similar vault designs. Although PALENCIA CATHEDRAL (1321–1514) was begun first, early in the fourteenth century, the interior took almost two centuries to complete and is thus similar in style to Salamanca and Segovia.[114] Juan Gil de Hontañón, along with his son Rodrigo Gil de Hontañón, had a hand in the design of both the NEW CATHEDRAL (1512–38) in Salamanca (built adjacent to the Romanesque Old Cathedral) and the SEGOVIA CATHEDRAL (1522–1768)

SAN JUAN DE LOS REYES (*see p. 144*)
SANTA MARÍA DEL PARRAL (*see p. 146*)
BURGOS CATHEDRAL (*see p. 147*)
CATHEDRAL OF SANTA MARIA (*see p. 149*)
PALENCIA CATHEDRAL (*see p. 150*)

NEW CATHEDRAL (*see p. 151*)
SEGOVIA CATHEDRAL (*see p. 153*)

choir (1563–91), which have almost identical star vault patterns.[115] In both cases the bay divisions are strongly defined by the transverse ribs and centralizing, circular petal-like liernes. Without these circular vault motifs, the circular crossing domes later added to both cathedrals would seem even more out of place.

Late Gothic architecture can be seen as the culmination of a progressive evolution of the Gothic rib toward pure texture. The highly detailed late Gothic rib patterns of vaults in Spain, England, and Germany seem to flow organically like rampant plant growth to cover the vault's entire surface. This quality of vegetal growth evokes the occasionally expressed analogy of the Gothic church as a garden or forest. The botanical association is an old one, reinforced by the sculptural foliage decoration, which also occurs in many churches, such as the capitals at Reims Cathedral, suggesting the symbolism of the church as the Garden of Paradise.[116]

Segovia Cathedral was the last great Gothic church built in Spain, ending the dominance of the Gothic style for more than four hundred years of European architecture. At the same time that the late Gothic cathedrals were being built at Palencia, Salamanca, and Segovia, St. Peter's Cathedral in Rome was being rebuilt in the classical style of the Renaissance, whose return to basic Roman forms was in part a conservative reaction to the elaborate detailing of late Gothic decoration. Renaissance architects favored the simple perfection of the circle and its derivations, the semicircular arch and the hemispherical dome, and denigrated the pointed arch of the Gothic builders, thinking it originated in the rustic huts of the northern forests. It must be remembered, though, that Filippo Brunelleschi, sometimes credited with the beginnings of the Italian Renaissance, is best known for his construction of the huge, pointed, octagonal dome over the crossing of the Gothic Basilica di Santa Maria del Fiore in Florence. In fact, many Renaissance architects were involved with the completion of Gothic buildings.

The use of the word *gothic*, or *gotiche*, to mean rustic or boorish, may first appear in a text by Leon Battista Alberti, one of the key Renaissance theorists. The word refers to the Visigoths or Goths, who under Alaric sacked Rome in the year 410, thus not endearing themselves to the Italians. Over the course of the Renaissance and later, the term came to refer to art and architecture from anywhere to the north of Italy—particularly Germany and France—considered to be uncouth, or decadent, in comparison to the simplified and idealized circular motifs so favored by the Italian Renaissance designers.[117] Of course, the successive phases of baroque and rococo architecture reintroduced increasingly complex decoration.

Gothic architecture enjoyed a renewal of interest in the nineteenth century, escaping its pejorative associations and spawning a range of highly decorative Gothic revival derivations. Some of the botanical sensibility of the late Gothic period also had an enduring legacy in early modernist idioms like art nouveau architecture. An echo of the Gothic vault system of skeletonized reinforcing ribs can even be seen in some of the most innovative contemporary steel and concrete architecture, although the virtuosity of Gothic stone masonry techniques is gone forever.

Every Gothic church represents a solution by its creators to a range of spiritual, liturgical, political, economic, structural, and aesthetic problems. Though the remoteness of these concerns makes the understanding of them difficult for us today, we can relate to the great Gothic churches as some of the most compelling art ever produced, still capable of providing an all-encompassing, transcendent experience.

Endnotes

1   Christopher Wilson, *The Gothic Cathedral: The Architecture of the Great Church 1130–1530* (London: Thames and Hudson, 1990), 8.

2   For a complete overview of this see Earl Baldwin Smith, *The Dome and Its Origins* (Princeton: Princeton University Press, 1972); and Karl Lehmann, "The Dome of Heaven," *Art Bulletin 27* (March 1945): 4.

3   Rolf Toman, ed., *Gothic* (Cologne: Konemann, 1998), 155.

4   Ibid., 154.

5   For a complete overview of medieval construction techniques see John Fitchen, *The Construction of Gothic Cathedrals: A Study of Medieval Vault Erection* (Chicago: University of Chicago Press, 1981).

6   Robert Mark, ed., *Architectural Technology up to the Scientific Revolution* (Cambridge, MA: MIT Press, 1993), 8–9.

7   Ibid., 142–44.

8   Paul Frankl, *Gothic Architecture*, rev. ed., rev. Paul Crossley (New Haven: Yale University Press, 2000), 44. Also, Marco Bussagli, ed., *Rome: Art and Architecture* (Cologne: Konemann, 1999), 418.

9   Mark, *Architectural Technology*, 145–47.

10   For a complete overview of this see David Stephenson, *Visions of Heaven: The Dome in European Architecture*, (New York: Princeton Architectural Press, 2005).

11   Kenneth John Conant, *Carolingian and Romanesque Architecture 800 to 1200* (Harmondsworth, UK: Penguin Books, 1966), 171–72.

12   Ibid., 231–32.

13   Ibid., 221.

14   Ibid., 98–103.

15   Ibid., 109, 113, 119–20.

16   Wilson, *The Gothic Cathedral*, 48.

17   Ibid., 76, 255–57.

18   Rolf Toman, ed., *Romanesque* (Cologne: Konemann, 1997), 7.

19   Wilson, *The Gothic Cathedral*, 48.

20   Conant, *Carolingian and Romanesque Architecture*, 126–29.

21 Frankl, *Gothic Architecture*, 53–54.

22 Ibid., 41–50.

23 Ibid.

24 For a complete discussion of Abbot Suger's views on light see Von Simson, *The Gothic Cathedral*.

25 Frankl, *Gothic Architecture*, 126; Wilson, *The Gothic Cathedral*, 31–42.

26 Frankl, *Gothic Architecture*, 84; Wilson, *The Gothic Cathedral*, 40–41.

27 Frankl, *Gothic Architecture*, 74–75.

28 Ibid., 60–65; Toman, *Gothic*, 36–38.

29 Frankl, *Gothic Architecture*, 82.

30 John Harvey, *English Mediaeval Architects* (Gloucester: Alan Sutton, 1984), 100–101.

31 Toman, *Gothic*, 123–25.

32 Ibid., 78–82; Harvey, *English Mediaeval Architects*, 185.

33 Toman, *Gothic*, 266.

34 Ibid., 98; Conant, *Carolingian and Romanesque Architecture*, 132–33; Frankl, *Gothic Architecture*, 216.

35 Frankl, *Gothic Architecture*, 101.

36 Wilson, *The Gothic Cathedral*, 48.

37 Frankl, *Gothic Architecture*, 105–108; Wilson, *The Gothic Cathedral*, 93–100.

38 Robert Mark, *Experiments in Gothic Structure* (Cambridge, MA: MIT Press, 1982), 34–49.

39 Frankl, *Gothic Architecture*, 108–11; Wilson, *The Gothic Cathedral*, 99, 108–12.

40 Mark, *Experiments in Gothic Structure*, 34–49.

41 Frankl, *Gothic Architecture*, 112; Wilson, *The Gothic Cathedral*, 99–101.

42 Adolf K. Placzek, ed., *Macmillan Encyclopedia of Architects*, vol. 2 (New York: The Free Press, 1982), 481–82; Frankl, *Gothic Architecture*, 114–15; Wilson, *The Gothic Cathedral*, 102–105.

43 Placzek, *Macmillan Encylopedia of Architects*, vol. 3, 587–88.

44 Frankl, *Gothic Architecture*, 119–23; Wilson, *The Gothic Cathedral*, 112–14.

45 Frankl, *Gothic Architecture*, 127–29.

46 Mark, *Experiments in Gothic Structure*, 58–75.

47 Toman, *Gothic*, 66.

48 Frankl, *Gothic Architecture*, 161–64; Wilson, *The Gothic Cathedral*, 124–25.

49 Frankl, *Gothic Architecture*, 130–32.

50 Ibid., 166–68; Wilson, *The Gothic Cathedral*, 126–27.

51 John Harvey, *The English Cathedrals* (London: Batsford, 1956), 168.

52 Harvey, *English Mediaeval Architects*, 94.

53 Frankl, *Gothic Architecture*, 123–25; Wilson, *The Gothic Cathedral*, 174–78.

54 Frankl, *Gothic Architecture*, 101.

55 Ibid., 146.

56 Harvey, *The English Cathedrals*, 164; *English Mediaeval Architects*, 286.

57 Harvey, *The English Cathedrals*, 160.

58 Ibid., 164.

59 Ibid., 170.

60 Frankl, *Gothic Architecture*, 158–59.

61 Ibid., 183.

62 Ibid., 155–56.

63 Ibid., 186.

64 Giandomenico Romanelli, ed., *Venice: Art and Architecture* (Cologne: Konemann, 1997), 151–54.

65 Ibid., 152–53.

66 Wilson, *The Gothic Cathedral*, 279; Toman, *Gothic*, 267–68.

67 Toman, *Gothic*, 179–82.

68 Wilson, *The Gothic Cathedral*, 156.

69 Toman, *Gothic*, 179–82.

70 Wilson, *The Gothic Cathedral*, 78–82, 199–203; Harvey, *The English Cathedrals*, 170.

71 Geoffrey Webb, *Architecture in Britain: The Middle Ages* (Harmondsworth, UK: Penguin Books, 1965), 154.

72 Ibid., 40; Harvey, *The English Cathedrals*, 166.

73 Frankl, *Gothic Architecture*, 177–78; Harvey, *The English Cathedrals*, 160.

74 Harvey, *English Mediaeval Architects*, 80.

75 Frankl, *Gothic Architecture*, 189; John Harvey, *The Perpendicular Style* (London: Batsford, 1978), 47, 77.

76 Harvey, *English Mediaeval Architects*, 164–65.

77 Frankl, *Gothic Architecture*, 83, 189; Wilson, *The Gothic Cathedral*, 78–82; Jean Bony, *The English Decorated Style: Gothic Architecture Transformed 1250–1350* (Oxford: Phaidon, 1979), 51.

78 Frankl, *Gothic Architecture*, 189; Harvey, *The Perpendicular Style*, 225–26; Bony, *The English Decorated Style*, 61.

79 Harvey, *English Mediaeval Architects*, 239–45.

80 Bony, *The English Decorated Style*, 59.

81 Harvey, *The English Cathedrals*, 174; *English Mediaeval Architects*, 156, 185.

82 Ibid.

83 Harvey, *The Perpendicular Style*, 121; *English Mediaeval Architects*, 358–66; Bony, *The English Decorated Style*, 61.

84 Harvey, *The Perpendicular Style*, 221.

85 Harvey, *The English Cathedrals*, 169–70.

86 Wilson, *The Gothic Cathedral*, 83–90; Harvey, *The Perpendicular Style*, 229; Harvey, *The English Cathedrals*, 157.

87 Toman, *Gothic*, 192–96.

88 Wilson, *The Gothic Cathedral*, 155–56.

89 Toman, *Gothic*, 196–97.

90 Frankl, *Gothic Architecture*, 200–204.

91 Ibid., 208.

92 Ibid., 223.

93 Ibid., 222–23; Toman, *Gothic*, 212–14.

94 Frankl, *Gothic Architecture*, 194–95, 235–36; Toman, *Gothic*, 205–206.

95 Frankl, *Gothic Architecture*, 206.

96 Ibid., 227, 229–30.

97 Ibid., 248.

98 Ibid., 253–54.

99 Ibid., 204, 253.

100 Ibid., 220.

101 Ibid., 237; James H. Acland, *Medieval Structure: The Gothic Vault* (Buffalo, NY: University of Toronto Press, 1972), 235.

102 Zoë Opacic, *Diamond Vaults: Innovation and Geometry in Medieval Architecture* (London: Architectural Association, 2005), 4.

103 Acland, *Medieval Structure*, 233–34; Randall Van Vynckt, ed., *International Dictionary of Architects and Architecture*, vol. 2 (Detroit: St. James Press, 1993), 159–60.

104 Harvey, *The English Cathedrals*, 165; *English Mediaeval Architects*, 102–103.

105 Harvey, *The English Cathedrals*, 165–66; *English Mediaeval Architects*, 220–23.

106 Harvey, *The English Cathedrals*, 155; *English Mediaeval Architects*, 305–10.

107 Harvey, *English Mediaeval Architects*, 316–25.

108 Frankl, *Gothic Architecture*, 216.

109 Toman, *Gothic*, 289–94; Frankl, *Gothic Architecture*, 251–52.

110 Frankl, *Gothic Architecture*, 251; Toman, *Gothic*, 295–98; Van Vynckt, *International Dictionary of Architects and Architecture*, vol 2, 750–52.

111 Frankl, *Gothic Architecture*, 239; Wilson, *The Gothic Cathedral*, 288–89; Toman, *Gothic*, 280–81.

112 Wilson, *The Gothic Cathedral*, 287.

113 Toman, *Gothic*, 276–77.

114 Ibid., 288.

115 Frankl, *Gothic Architecture*, 255–56; Wilson, *The Gothic Cathedral*, 290–319.

116 Frankl, *Gothic Architecture*, 275.

117 Paul Frankl, *The Gothic: Literary Sources and Interpretations through Eight Centuries* (Princeton: Princeton University Press, 1960), 257–59.

BIBLIOGRAPHY

Acland, James H. *Medieval Structure: The Gothic Vault*. Buffalo, NY: University of Toronto Press, 1972.

Bony, Jean. *The English Decorated Style: Gothic Architecture Transformed 1250–1350*. Oxford: Phaidon, 1979.

———. *French Gothic Architecture of the 12th and 13th Centuries*. Berkeley: University of California Press, 1983.

Bussagli, Marco, ed. *Rome: Art and Architecture*. Cologne: Konemann, 1999.

Conant, Kenneth John. *Carolingian and Romanesque Architecture 800 to 1200*. Harmondsworth, UK: Penguin Books, 1966.

Fitchen, John. *The Construction of Gothic Cathedrals: A Study of Medieval Vault Erection*. Chicago: University of Chicago Press, 1981.

Frankl, Paul. *Gothic Architecture*. Rev. ed. Revised by Paul Crossley. New Haven: Yale University Press, 2000. First published 1962 by Penguin Books.

Harvey, John. *The English Cathedrals*. London: Batsford, 1956.

———. *English Mediaeval Architects*. Gloucester: Alan Sutton, 1984.

———. *The Perpendicular Style*. London: Batsford, 1978.

Krautheimer, Richard. *Early Christian and Byzantine Architecture*. Harmondsworth, UK: Penguin Books, 1965.

Kubler, George, and Martin Soria. *Art and Architecture in Spain and Portugal and their American Dominions 1500 to 1800*. Harmondsworth, UK: Penguin Books, 1959.

Lehmann, Karl. "The Dome of Heaven." *Art Bulletin* 27 (March 1945): 4.

Mark, Robert, ed. *Architectural Technology up to the Scientific Revolution*. Cambridge, MA: MIT Press, 1993.

———. *Experiments in Gothic Structure*. Cambridge, MA: MIT Press, 1982.

———. *Light, Wind, and Structure: The Mystery of the Master Builders*. Cambridge, MA: MIT Press, 1990.

Opacic, Zoë. *Diamond Vaults: Innovation and Geometry in Medieval Architecture*. London: Architectural Association, 2005.

Placzek, Adolf K., ed. *Macmillan Encyclopedia of Architecture*. New York: The Free Press, 1982.

Romanelli, Giandomenico, ed. *Venice: Art and Architecture*. Cologne: Konemann, 1997.

Shepard, Paul. *Man in the Landscape*. New York: Ballantine, 1972.

Smith, Earl Baldwin. *The Dome and Its Origins*. Princeton: Princeton University Press, 1972.

Stephenson, David. *Visions of Heaven: The Dome in European Architecture*. New York: Princeton Architectural Press, 2005.

Stierlin, Henri. *Islam: Early Architecture from Baghdad to Cordoba*. Cologne: Taschen, 1996.

Toman, Rolf, ed. *Gothic*. Cologne: Konemann, 1998.

———, ed. *Romanesque*. Cologne: Konemann, 1997.

Van Vynckt, Randall, ed. *International Dictionary of Architects and Architecture*. Detroit: St. James Press, 1993.

Von Simson, Otto. *The Gothic Cathedral: Origins of Gothic Architecture and the Medieval Concept of Order*. New York: Bolligen Foundation, 1962.

Viollet-le-Duc, Eugène Emmanuel. *Dictionnaire raisonne de l'architecture francaise du XIe au XVIe siecle*. Paris: B. Bance, 1858–1868.

Webb, Geoffrey. *Architecture in Britain: The Middle Ages*. Harmondsworth, UK: Penguin Books, 1965.

White, John. *Art and Architecture in Italy 1250 to 1400*. Harmondsworth, UK: Penguin Books, 1966.

Wilson, Christopher. *The Gothic Cathedral: The Architecture of the Great Church 1130–1530*. London: Thames and Hudson, 1990.

ACKNOWLEDGMENTS

I owe a great debt to a number of individuals and organizations for both material and intellectual support with this project. Foremost are the builders of the churches themselves, as well as the organizations that have continued to maintain the buildings and allow visitors access.

As I am an artist rather than an art historian, my research relies heavily on the work of a number of architectural scholars, who are credited in the references and bibliography. I have tried to balance their differing accounts and my personal experience of each building. Any errors that remain, however, are solely mine.

I am deeply grateful to the Australia Council for the Arts for their grant of an artist's fellowship during 2008 and 2009, which has allowed me to take time away from my teaching duties to complete this project and others.

I thank the Tasmanian School of Art at the University of Tasmania and my colleagues there, particularly Professor of Art and Head of School Noel Frankham, for their ongoing support of my work. In 2006 a University of Tasmania outside studies program assisted my initial research on Gothic vaults in France, Belgium, and England. Photography Technical Officer Gerrard Dixon cheerfully maintained the color print processor and executed the many reproduction scans.

For exhibiting this project in its preliminary phases and continuing to support my work, I thank Julie Saul Gallery in New York; Bett Gallery in Hobart, Australia; Boutwell Draper Gallery in Sydney; and John Buckley Gallery in Melbourne.

Isobel Crombie, senior curator of photography at the National Gallery of Victoria in Melbourne, has been a longtime supporter, and I am grateful particularly for her generous and insightful foreword.

As with my previous book, *Visions of Heaven*, Princeton Architectural Press, and particularly my editor, Nicola Bednarek, have been the model of cheerful competence, making the whole process of bringing a book to fruition far more enjoyable than it might otherwise be. Their support of the vaults project from its infancy is deeply appreciated.

Finally, I am forever grateful for the patience, love, and support of both my wife Anne MacDonald—always an astute critic of my work—and our son Zachary, who teaches me every day the meaning of discovery.